VICTOR HUGO
and his world

dessiné d'après nature par

Maurin

VICTOR HUGO
and his world

BY ANDRÉ MAUROIS

A STUDIO BOOK

THE VIKING PRESS · NEW YORK

Translated from the French by Oliver Bernard

Text based on Olympio, The Life of Victor Hugo
© 1956 by André Maurois with the permission of Harper and Row Publishers

Published in 1966 by The Viking Press, Inc.
625 Madison Avenue, New York, N.Y. 10022

Library of Congress catalog card number: 66–14093

Printed in Great Britain by Jarrold and Sons Ltd, Norwich, England

CONTENTS

Mme Joseph-Léopold-Sigisbert
Hugo (born Françoise Trébuchet),
Victor Hugo's mother

General Hugo, the writer's father

Mme Trébuchet (born Lenormand du Buisson), Victor Hugo's maternal grandmother

ABOUT 1770 THERE LIVED IN NANCY a master-carpenter, Joseph Hugo, who enjoyed driftwood rights on the Moselle and owned, apart from his capital, a few small properties in the town. The family name, German in origin, was common in Lorraine. In the sixteenth century a certain Georges Hugo had been a captain in the Guards, and had later been ennobled; there had also been a Louis Hugo, Abbot of Estival, and later Bishop of Ptolémaïs. Was there perhaps a family connexion between the bishop and the carpenter? No one knew, but the carpenter's children liked to think there was, and would tell the story of how Françoise Hugo, Comtesse de Graffigny, used to write letters to their father beginning: 'Dear cousin'. Joseph Hugo had seven daughters by his first wife, Dieudonnée Béchet, and by his second, Jeanne-Marguerite Michaud, five sons – all of whom enlisted in the revolutionary armies. Two of them were killed at Wissembourg; the other three became officers.

The old quai de Battant in Besançon, demolished in 1865

The third son, Joseph-Léopold-Sigisbert Hugo, was born at Nancy on 15 November 1773. His thick hair, growing rather too low on his forehead, his prominent eyes, snub nose, thick and sensual lips and ruddy complexion would have made his face seem coarse, had not a look of kindness, a sparkle of intelligence in his eyes, and a sweetness in his smile made it an attractive one. His studies, begun with the Canons Regular at Nancy, were soon interrupted by his enlistment at the age of fifteen. In 1792, as a young captain in the Army of the Rhine, he became acquainted with the battalion commander, Kléber, Lieutenant Desaix, and General Alexandre de Beauharnais, Josephine's first husband. A gallant soldier, he was wounded several times, and had two horses killed under him. In 1793 he was sent to put down the revolt in the Vendée, and was promoted to major.

Léopold Hugo, who owed everything to the Revolution, shared its passions to the point of signing his letters: 'The sans-culotte Brutus Hugo.' But his heart was still human, and 'Charette's brigands' were quick to learn that this 'Blue' was not without pity. Perhaps indeed his reputation for mercy was responsible for the kind reception given to him, a republican officer, by a Breton girl, Sophie Trébuchet, at the manor-farm of la Renaudière, at Petit-Auverné, when he called there to ask for an hour's shelter for his worn-out men.

This young person, neat, pretty, with large brown eyes in an energetic and almost haughty face, was one of the three daughters of a ship's captain from Nantes who had once been a slave-trader, and the grand-daughter on her mother's side, of a public prosecutor of the Presidial of Nantes, M. Lenormand du Buisson.

Orphaned in childhood, Sophie had been brought up by an aunt, an intelligent woman, a royalist and a Voltairean, whose ideas the young girl had adopted. The young captain did not however displease her. He had rescued women, children, hostages. She took a certain pleasure in walking with him in the sunken lanes of the Bocage, and in spiritedly expounding to him the injustice of the war against the Chouans. Hugo defended the actions of the Republic with vigour, but admired the firm character of this young and attractive woman. This discordant idyll was short-lived; the 8th Battalion of the Lower Rhine Regiment was recalled to Paris by the Directory. Nevertheless Hugo, in Paris, did not forget 'his little Sophie of Châteaubriant' but continued to write to her. He proposed marriage.

Victor Hugo's birth-
place in Besançon

9

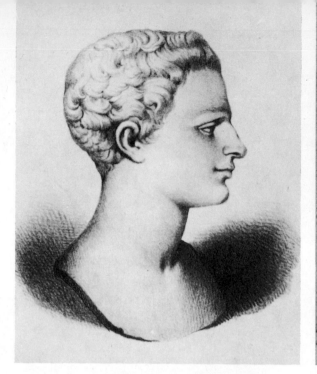

Eugène Hugo, Victor's senior
by two years

Abel, born in 1798, was the eldest of the
three brothers, and acted the part

She was alone in the world, and seventeen months his senior; she needed support. She arrived in Paris with her brother. Hugo 'made her dizzy with his praises', and on 15 November 1797 they went through a civil marriage ceremony at the town hall of the 9th arrondissement, in the Fidélité quarter.

The couple spent two years in Paris; he very much in love with his clever Breton girl, she a little fatigued by her husband's loquaciousness and broad jokes, and worn out by the ardours of this bull-necked man. Yet she remained secretive, tenacious and dominating.

In 1798 the Hugos had a son, Abel, and in the following year the major rejoined his unit. At first he left his wife at Nancy. Pregnant for the second time and vaguely in love with another man, Sophie was more alarmed than ever by the extent of her husband's ardour. Seeking a rest from conjugal life, she asked in letters—which the major, whose epistolary style was warmth and gallantry itself, found 'icy' – for her confinement to be allowed to take place in Brittany. This hostile attitude made the young husband desperate. However, after the birth of her second son Eugène, she was obliged to join her husband at Lunéville, of which town he had been appointed governor.

*Birth of
Victor Hugo*

In 1801, thanks to an excursion into the mountains on the journey from Lunéville to Besançon, a third Hugo offspring was conceived. This third child, a son, was born at Besançon on 26 February 1802, in a house which dated from the seventeenth century. His parents asked General Victor Lahorie to be the boy's godfather and Marie Dessirier, wife of Jacques Delelée, the brigade commander in charge of the garrison at Besançon, to be his godmother; hence his Christian names: Victor Marie. But the child seemed so puny that the doctor thought its survival impossible.

Six weeks after the birth of his third son, Hugo received orders to proceed to Marseilles to take command of a battalion which was about to leave for Santo Domingo.

Believing himself to be the victim of persecution, and in great danger, he foolishly sent his young wife to Paris in order to plead with Joseph Bonaparte and with Generals Clarke and Lahorie to rescue him from his enemies by a change of posting. Sophie, although sad at the thought of leaving her three boys, agreed to go to Paris.

In June 1803, Victor, aged sixteen months, was, according to the major, calling for his 'mamaman'. He had a huge head, which was too large for his body, and made him look like a misshapen dwarf. 'He would be found in corners, weeping silently for no apparent reason. . . .' One can imagine what was going on in the heart of this motherless child, the feeble last-born of the three brothers. Thus it was that a melancholic strain developed in his character – a strain which overcame his prodigious vitality from time to time throughout his life.

In 1803 the battalion left for Elba, and it was there, at Porto-Ferrajo, that Mme Hugo at last rejoined her family. She knew exactly what she wanted to do: take her three sons, whom she adored, back with her to Paris, and there rejoin her beloved Lahorie. She left in November 1803. Her stay in Porto-Ferrajo had lasted less than four months.

Victor Hugo's earliest memories were of the house in the rue de Clichy. He remembered 'how his mother sent him to the school in the rue du Mont-Blanc; how he would be taken in the morning into the room in which Mlle Rose, the schoolmaster's daughter, slept; how Mlle Rose, still in bed, would make him sit on the bed near her; and how, when she got up, he would watch her pulling her stockings on. . . .' In the meantime, Léopold Hugo had gone to Italy. Gentle Joseph Bonaparte, the man of letters transformed, in spite of himself, into a man of war by his famous brother, had received orders to conquer the kingdom of Naples. Major Hugo was known to this prince – he had served under him at Lunéville – and Joseph was well disposed towards him. Sophie no longer concerned herself with this distant, almost non-existent husband, except to ask him for money. He sent her half his pay, though not without grumbling.

Childhood

Now at last Hugo had an opportunity to distinguish himself, and Joseph appointed him Governor of the province of Avellino, and promoted him to Colonel of the Royal-Corse.

But about this time (1807) Lahorie's situation worsened. When Sophie Hugo saw that her friend, hounded by his adversary Fouché, could no longer come

Victor Hugo in 1819, the year of the publication of his first ode and declaration of love for Adèle Foucher

to Paris, and that there was going to be a shortage of money for her sons, she decided to return to her husband. It was the law of necessity. Sophie did not pay any attention to her husband's protests. In October 1807 she started out for Italy without warning him of her decision.

Little Victor was only five, but he was a sensitive and observant child. He was never to forget this journey by stage-coach across France.

Every child lives in a fairyland, but the fairyland of Victor Hugo's first years seems to have been especially colourful. In Italy the three brothers lived in a dilapidated marble palace, near which there was a deep ravine, shaded by hazel trees. No more school; complete freedom. It was a holiday atmosphere the memory of which Victor would love all his life. An all-powerful father, who was hardly ever to be seen, appeared from time to time and sat on his big sword to amuse his sons, but was always respectfully attended in the courtyard by horsemen with polished helmets; this was the father whom the King of Naples, the Emperor's brother, loved; the father who had had little Victor's name inscribed on the muster-roll of the Royal-Corse – from that moment Victor considered himself a soldier.

There had been no reconciliation between the colonel and his wife. The children were vaguely aware of mysterious quarrels whose causes they did not understand. They were proud of their father and yet conscious of some offence committed by him against their adored mother. In any case they would not have been able to stay long in Naples, because soon after their departure Colonel Hugo was ordered to Madrid by Joseph Bonaparte who had been promised the crown 'of Spain and the Indies'. Léopold Hugo had given up the idea of winning back his wife, if not of protecting his children.

The Hermitage of the Feuillantines, 12 impasse des Feuillantines, one of Victor Hugo's first homes in Paris

Napoleon's brother, Joseph Bonaparte, King of Naples and later King of Spain and the Indies

February 1809, Paris. Mme Hugo, who was now assured of an allowance of three thousand francs, soon increased to four thousand, found an enormous apartment at 12 impasse des Feuillantines, on the ground floor of the former convent founded by Anne of Austria. 'I see myself as a child again, a fresh, smiling schoolboy, playing, running, laughing with my brothers in the great green avenue of that garden in which I passed my earliest years, a place which had once been a nuns' private garden, dominated by the dark leaden dome of the Val-de-Grâce . . .' the poet would write later, in *Le Dernier Jour d'un Condamné*.

Léopold-Sigisbert Hugo had become a general in King Joseph's army, as well as an important member of his court, and Count of Siguenza (a Spanish title). The king heaped honours and bounties on him. In the spring of 1811 Mme Hugo was advised that a convoy was being formed and that she must join it at Bayonne. She loathed travelling. For her sons, however, the news was intoxicating. They loved riding in carriages, seeing town after town. Victor's eye was so keen and his memory so faithful that twenty years later he would be able to draw the two fine towers of Angoulême Cathedral of which he had only caught a glimpse. And all his life he would remember Bayonne, where they had to wait a month for the convoy. Victor liked Spain immediately; it was a land of contrasts. His eyes, accustomed to star-spangled beds, swan-necked armchairs, fire-dogs in the shape of sphinxes, ormolu, beheld with a kind of terror the testered beds, the heavy and elaborate silver plate and the leaded lattice-windows. But this very terror pleased him.

From the time of this journey the young Victor Hugo would be haunted by spectres, nameless as yet, which would become Hernani, Ruy Gomez de Silva, Don Salluste and Ruy Blas; by images of blood and gold; and by a 'little Spanish girl with big eyes and a great head of hair, golden-brown skin, red lips and pink cheeks, the fourteen year old Andalusian Pepa. . . .' From this short but intimate contact with Spain he was to retain a taste for sonorous words and emphatic feelings.

All three brothers, Abel, Eugène and Victor, wrote poetry. Victor filled exercise books full of it. His thoughts adapted themselves naturally to classical rhythms. Mme Hugo presided without effort over the minds of her sons. She demanded and obtained respect, punctuality and obedience.

In 1813 General Hugo, following the defeat of Joseph Bonaparte, was obliged to return to France. September found him at Pau, together with Abel and the woman whom Mme Hugo sometimes called 'the Thomas woman' and sometimes 'the alleged Comtesse de Salcano'. Though a general in Spain, Léopold-Sigisbert Hugo was still only a battalion commander in France, and the allowance promised to his wife was not paid.

General Hugo asked to be recalled to active duty. He was given command of the fortified town of Thionville on 9 January 1814. He defended it bravely against invasion and capitulated only when he heard of Napoleon I's abdication. Abel had rejoined his mother in Paris. She was proud of this handsome, broad-shouldered young man. General Hugo remained at his post in Thionville until May 1814. His wife, accompanied by Abel, travelled there to claim her allowance. Their incompatibility had become hatred. The general wished to rescue his sons from this 'abhorred' wife, and when he arrived in Paris in September 1814, he boarded Victor and Eugène, as his rights as a father allowed him to do, at Cordier and Decotte's school, in the rue Sainte-Marguerite, 'a sombre passageway hemmed in between the Abbaye prison and the passage du Dragon'. When in March 1815 he was recalled to Thionville to defend the town once more against the new invasion, he delegated his paternal authority to his sister, the shrewish widow of Martin-Chopine. The two boys immediately came into open rebellion against this woman. They called her Madame instead of Aunt. Both of them remained completely devoted to the mother from whom they had been separated. After the paradise of the Feuillantines Cordier and Decotte's, gloomy and without a single green leaf, resembled a dreary purgatory. They acquired from the outset a marked prestige among their companions because their father had insisted on separate sleeping-quarters for them. The school divided itself into two camps, the one choosing Victor for its king, the other Eugène. In the evening the rival monarchs would meet in the room they shared and negotiate. It was reminiscent of the brothers Bonaparte and their sharing

The cour du Dragon, next to Cordier and Decotte's school, where Victor Hugo and his brothers were boarders from 1814 to 1818

out of Europe; and no doubt the brothers Hugo were not unmindful of the parallel.

Both did homage in their verses to their mother who, being unable to have her sons living with her, used to visit them at the school. The note-books which have been preserved from this time contain thousands of verses; a complete comic opera; a prose melodrama, *Inez de Castro*; a sketch for a verse tragedy in five acts, *Athélie ou les Scandinaves,* and an epic poem, *Le Déluge* – all illustrated, in the margins, with drawings whose intricacy and boldness occasionally recall those of Rembrandt. It should be added that at the same time Victor was reading for the Polytechnique examination, that he was getting high marks in science, and that from the end of 1816, with Eugène, two years his elder, he attended lectures at the college of Louis-le-Grand, from eight in the morning to five in the afternoon. To write verse he had to use part of the night, and he worked by candlelight in his attic. It was like an oven in June and like an ice-box in December, and from it he could see the semaphore on the towers of Saint-Sulpice. An injury to his knee, which kept him in bed for several weeks, allowed him to devote himself even more to the occupation he loved.

Victor kept a frank and intimate journal. On 10 July 1816 at the age of fourteen, he wrote: 'I want to be Chateaubriand or nothing.' A choice which is easy to understand. Since 1789 France, drunk on Roman rhetoric, had been seeking greatness. On this point, for the first time, Victor disagreed with his mother. He for his part admired *Atala*, of which she, a woman of the eighteenth century, was reading and enjoying a stupid parody, *Ah! là là!* It is improbable that Chateaubriand would have seen Victor Hugo's first literary attempts.

On 3 February 1818 occurred an event of the very greatest importance; the Hugos were legally separated. 'Mme Trébuchet' obtained custody of the children, with an allowance of three thousand francs. In August the two brothers took an ecstatic leave of Cordier and Decotte's and went to live with their mother at 18 rue des Petits-Augustine (now rue Bonaparte).

There is nothing finer than a mother's confidence in the genius of her children. It did not even occur to Mme Hugo to oblige her sons to actually study law. That agreement between her and the general was just 'a scrap of paper'. In fact, although Eugène and Victor kept their names on the books for two years, they neither attended lectures nor sat for examinations. Already proud of their expected triumphs, she wished to turn her sons neither into advocates nor into civil servants, but into great writers. Nothing less. Every evening they walked as far as the rue du Cherche-Midi, where Pierre Foucher, a department head at the Ministry of War, lived at the Hôtel de Toulouse.

Adèle Foucher

There would be Mme Foucher, a sweet, pious and still youthful lady, and her daughter Adèle, a Spanish type of beauty, who had once been the Hugos' playmate. *Tres para una.* They could hardly believe that ten years ago at the Feuillantines they had given this adorable girl rides in a wheelbarrow and played with her on the swing.

Adèle Foucher, who
married Victor Hugo
in 1822

Pierre Foucher,
Adèle's father

One day when she was alone with Victor under the great chestnut tree she said to him: 'You must have secrets; haven't you got one which is bigger than all the others?' He agreed. 'So have I', she said; 'well then, listen! Tell me your greatest secret, and I'll tell you mine.' 'My great secret', said Victor, 'is that I love you.' 'My great secret is that I love you', replied the girl. This took place on 26 April 1819. They were both of them shy and well-behaved; he ardent and serious, she very pious. This attachment remained perfectly innocent and was all the stronger for that. 'After your answer, my Adèle, I felt as brave as a lion.'

Sophie Hugo's sense of maternal obligation amounted to possessiveness: she was jealous of her son and proud of him. She was certain that Victor was destined for a dazzling future. In addition he was the son of General Count Hugo. Was it possible that at eighteen years of age he should be about to ruin his life by marrying this little Foucher girl? The idea of swaying his mother did not even occur to him. Victor realized that she was 'unswerving and inexorable' and 'as intolerant in her hatreds as she was ardent in her affections'. Love thus escaped him, and he sought consolation in work. Abel decided that the three Hugo brothers should have their own magazine. Their master Chateaubriand's journal was called *Le Conservateur*; theirs would be known as *Le Conservateur littéraire*. It appeared from December 1819 until March 1821, and was written and edited mainly by Victor. One continues to be amazed, as one looks through this collection, by the intelligence and the erudition of this boy. Literary criticism, dramatic criticism, foreign literature – he speaks of everything with a wealth of reference indicating real cultural depth, especially in Latin and Greek.

Victor also attempted to express his love by writing a frenzied romance, *Han d'Islande*, in which he depicted himself under the name of Ordener, and Adèle under that of Ethel. *Han d'Islande*, an unfinished work, could not appear in *Le Conservateur littéraire*, which ceased publication in 1822, or to be more exact, was incorporated in *Annales de la Littérature et des Arts*. For magazines incorporation is the most honourable form of suicide. *Le Conservateur littéraire* had been a useful experience for the sublime child. There was in this young man more than just a great journalist, but he did possess, and always retained, the journalist's gift of being able to give dramatic intensity to everyday matters.

Unable to tolerate living in a third-floor flat without a garden, General Hugo's wife had moved in January 1821 to 10 rue de Mézières, a ground-floor apartment taken for her by Abel. Her sons, whom she had accustomed to working with their hands (besides being artisans by family tradition), became joiners, painters, decorators, dyers; their mother had no other resources for fitting out the apartment. Mme Hugo and her children dug, planted, grafted, raked and hoed. She exhausted herself, got too hot, caught a cold and suffered a serious inflammation of the lungs. Her sons spent whole nights looking after her. At three in the morning of 27 June she died in their arms.

An illustration showing the
heroes of *Han d'Islande*,
Victor Hugo's first novel

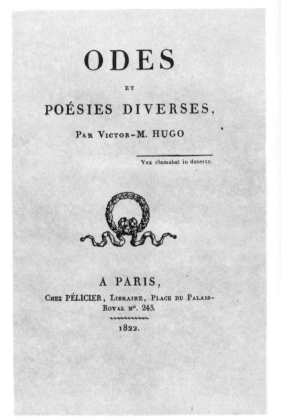

ODES

ET

POÉSIES DIVERSES,

Par Victor-M. HUGO

Vox clamabat in deserto.

A PARIS,

Chez PÉLICIER, Libraire, Place du Palais-
Royal n°. 243.

1822.

Cover of the first book
published by Hugo:
Odes et Poésies diverses (1822)

M. Foucher paid a visit of condolence to the rue de Mézières, and strongly
advised Victor to leave Paris. The cost of living there was high, and these
young men seemed very poor. Victor had written to tell his father the terrible
news.

The Fouchers said to each other that if they were to rent a house for the
summer, as they usually did, on the outskirts of Paris, young Hugo was sure to
come. They decided to go to Dreux. It was twenty-five francs from Paris by
stage-coach, and Victor did not possess twenty-five francs. But this was to
forget that he had something better than money: a will of iron and a taste for

Victor Hugo
aged twenty

adventure. The Fouchers and their daughter left by carriage on 15 July; Victor
followed on the 16th. The young people were in love. Pierre Foucher decided
that the engagement would not be announced and that he would not yet
receive Victor in his house, but that Adèle and her suitor should be allowed to
write to each other.

On 8 March 1822, spurred by Adèle, Victor at last decided to ask the General's
consent to marry. Adèle was shown the letter and thought it well enough, apart
from the angelic representation of herself which it contained. There followed
several days of anxious waiting. In the event of his father's refusal, they discussed fleeing together and marrying in some foreign country. On this occasion
the well-brought-up girl from the rue du Cherche-Midi accepted the challenge

of passion, a challenge which it was not necessary to take up, since the General's answer, prudent on the whole, was one of consent, subject to certain conditions: '... You must have some means of support or some post; and I cannot consider a literary career, however brilliantly begun, to constitute such a thing. Therefore when you have obtained one or the other of these things, you may expect me to comply with your wishes, wishes to which I am not in any case opposed ....'

And so Victor hurried on the publication of a volume of his *Odes*. It was the generous Abel who had them printed, and put on sale in Pélicier's bookshop in the place du Palais-Royal (he gave his brother a delightful surprise by sending him the 'proofs). The volume appeared in June, in greenish-grey covers. Fifteen hundred copies were printed. The author received fifty centimes per copy, or seven hundred and fifty francs in all. The first copy was suitably

The house the Fouchers, Victor Hugo's future parents-in-law, rented at Gentilly for the summer of 1822, the summer Adèle and Victor became engaged

Medallions by David d'Angers made after the wedding of Adèle and Victor Hugo

addressed, 'To my beloved Adèle, the angel who is all I desire of glory or possess of happiness – Victor.'

'Odes et Poésies diverses'

The title of this first book was *Odes et Poésies diverses*. Its preface emphasized the author's political aspirations. The royalist press itself, on which he was counting, hardly reacted. There were few reviews. At that time literary criticism occupied little space, and Hugo considered it 'unworthy of a self-respecting person to follow this fashion of begging fame from journalists . . . I shall send my book to the papers; they can discuss it if they are so minded, but I shall not seek their praises as one seeks alms. . . .' However, the sales were fairly encouraging, which brought the wedding nearer; and now Adèle was emboldened to the extent of visiting her fiancé, ill and all alone at his home in Paris: 'Never mind what they say. . . . There are circumstances in which I am happy to brave paternal sanctions. . . .' But they waited to be married before giving themselves to each other. *Adèle to Victor*: 'Three more months and I shall be near you always. . . . And when we remember that we have never done anything unworthy, and that we could have been together sooner, except that we preferred self-respect to happiness, how much happier, surely, we must be! . . .'

Marriage

The wedding was solemnized at Saint-Sulpice, on 12 October 1822, by the Abbé Duc de Rohan. The bridegroom's witnesses were Alfred de Vigny, and Félix Biscarrat, Victor's former teacher at Cordier's; the bride's were her uncle

The towers of Saint-Sulpice surmounted by Chappe's semaphore ▶

Jean-Baptiste Asseline and the Marquis Duvidal de Montferrier. General Hugo did not attend the ceremony.

There was a dinner at the Fouchers', then a ball in the great hall of the War Council building. During the evening Biscarrat, the young schoolmaster with the pock-marked face, noticed Eugène's unusual agitation. He seemed to be beside himself and was making extraordinary remarks. Avoiding attracting attention, Biscarrat warned Abel, and both of them removed the unfortunate young man. During the night he went raving mad. Always gloomy, believing himself persecuted, in love with Adèle and suffering from long-standing and appalling jealousy, he had been unable to bear the sight of his brother's happiness.

Luckily the young couple knew nothing of the tragedy that evening. For Victor, who was at the same time so chaste in his morals and so ardent in his imagination, it was intoxicating to possess at last this girl who in his eyes was the incarnation of beauty. A strong-minded mother had taught him that events could be mastered. What a distance he had travelled in a year! At twenty he was on the highroad to fame: read both by the ageing king and by the young men; he had been given a pension by the Ministry and he was respected by other poets. He had conquered by force of arms the woman of his choice, won back his father's affection, and imposed on everybody his choice of career. It seemed after so many misfortunes, like a happy dream full of love and mystery, or like a magician's granting of all a child's wishes. But the magician was himself. *Ego Hugo.*

His night of happiness had been well-earned. Even in that disappointing future, when Adèle became 'the Eve whom no fruit could tempt', Hugo would never forget that together, in a far-off day, they had tasted an almost super-human happiness. The Foucher girl was a young girl like any other, but just as she was, naïve, somewhat limited, artistic (her drawings bear witness to that), by no means a fool, but indifferent to poetry, Adèle had helped to bring a poet into the world.

In the morning a distraught Biscarrat knocked on the door of the wedding chamber. Eugène's condition was grave. The general was warned, and he at once undertook the journey from Blois to Paris. 'He had not come to take part in the happiness; but he wished to share in the grief.' Victor and Adèle affectionately welcomed this 'dear Papa' to whom they owed their union. 'Like frost in sunshine, the son's bitterness disappeared before the radiant kindness of this excellent man.'

To find the handsome Eugène, the chubby, blond lad he had known in Corsica and in Italy, the schoolboy who had shown such promise in Madrid, now in the grip of madness, was a painful experience. His terrible fate was, for Victor, a permanent cause for sadness and undefined remorse. Had not he himself, by triumphing over his brother in the field of poetry as well as that of love, reduced him to this despair? He had committed no crime, he was faultless,

General Hugo's house at Blois ▶

26

but it is a fact that the theme of enmity between brothers was to become one of his obsessions. In plays, poems, novels, in all forms he would return to it.

Of these dark internal fires nothing appeared on the surface. All those who knew him during these first months of his marriage noticed his conquering manner, his gait 'as of a cavalry officer storming a post'. Young as he was, he wanted his life to be that of a husband and father. 'A patriarchal atmosphere, at once lofty and idyllic, was spontaneously generated around him.' He would now have three persons to support. Léopold Hugo II was born punctually, nine months after the wedding, on 16 July 1823.

Work, work, work, above the great chestnut trees in the rue du Cherche-Midi. New odes were written. *Han d'Islande*, now completed, was sent to Persan, a marquis turned publisher, who signed a contract to reprint the *Odes* and to print a thousand copies of *Han d'Islande*. But Hugo received only five hundred francs of his royalties. Persan went bankrupt, and being unable to pay Hugo, calumniated him. That is the custom. Hugo's apprenticeship in the seamy side of letters had begun. Once more it was necessary to call on the general.

Han d'Islande appeared in four volumes, in grey covers on coarse paper and without the author's name. 'This unusual work', announced Persan, 'is understood to be the first prose work of a young man who is already well known for his brilliant successes as a poet.' It should be noted that parody and witticism

were not entirely absent from this accumulation of murders, monsters, gibbets, executioners and tortures. It was a *tour de force* in the horror genre.

Relations with General Hugo now became more and more affectionate. Father and son corresponded, first about Eugène, then about the father's desire for reinstatement and promotion.

General Hugo had two motives: he wished to lean upon his son who was now in official favour, and he wanted the second Mme Hugo who, he said 'will be a second mother to all of you', to be accepted by his sons. As it happened, when Victor's first son was born, after a difficult confinement, and when 'the poor little angel' seemed to be pining away, the general and his lady had him moved with his nurse to Blois, to the big white house they had just bought. The 'Thomas woman' was never called anything now but 'Léopold's grandmother'. Adèle embroidered a cap for her mother-in-law.

On 9 October, little Léopold died. But despite so many misfortunes – his mother, his brother, his son – Hugo did not find life sad; he was too busy living, working and making love. Once more Adèle found herself pregnant. 'Victor', said Émile Deschamps, 'produces odes and offspring without a moment's rest.'

Émile Deschamps proposed forming a group and founding a review. This was *La Muse française*, a group of distinguished, almost too distinguished, young men, lovers of poetry, and royalists by tradition. Their platform was: in religion, the Christianity of wonder in the manner of Chateaubriand, as against the licentious paganism of the Empire; in politics, the monarchy according to the Charter; in love, chivalrous Platonism. To establish *La Muse*, Émile Deschamps had suggested that everyone should contribute a thousand francs. It was too much for the Hugos' resources. Lamartine, who already preferred to remain detached from literary politics and to live the life of a country gentleman, far from the noisy world of letters, refused to be a part of the group, but offered to pay Hugo's subscription. In any case the good-hearted Nodier quickly became the real centre of the *Muse française* group. All these men, though colleagues, were good friends. The reign of graceful wit, as Émile Deschamps put it, was giving place to that of the noble heart. They were generous in their praises of each other. Most of the contributors to *La Muse française* felt that although they were restoring and renewing poetry, they ought not to take any part in the quarrel between Romanticism and Classicism.

'Nouvelles Odes'   When his *Nouvelles Odes* were published by the bookseller Ladvocat in March 1824, Victor Hugo in his preface was still unwilling to make a choice. He stood out against the view that the literary revolution was the expression of the political revolution of 1789. It was not in fact its expression, declared the young Hugo, but its result – which is quite a different matter.

Nothing is more difficult than to write, without padding or awkwardness, short lines which combine sense and rhythm. At twenty-two Hugo did it with masterly ease. But he was a Romantic without knowing it, and the critic of the

Victor Hugo's wife holding on her lap Léopoldine, her elder daughter

Journal des Débats denounced him, reproaching him with associating abstract ideas with physical images.

The Hugo finances strengthened. For two years' publication rights to the *Nouvelles Odes*, the bookseller Ladvocat paid two thousand francs. The general paid him a small monthly allowance, and Victor, who was now receiving two royal pensions, urged his father to consult 'his own convenience above all things in paying it'. The young couple had been able to move, in 1824, into a small flat above a joiner's shop at 90 rue de Vaugirard. They paid six hundred and twenty-five francs per annum in rent. Here, on 28 August, Léopoldine Hugo was born. 'Our "Didine" is lovely. She takes after her mother, and her grandfather. . . .' The countess, the general's wife, became her godmother. A tactful move.

Birth of Léopoldine

The rue de Vaugirard became a rallying-point for many young writers. The Hugo household was, in their eyes, ideal. Mme Victor shed the glow of her beauty over this calm interior, dedicated to work. The *Odes* appeared to the group to be the sweet and solemn echo of this 'chaste, solitary' existence.

Occasionally Lamartine would come to dine at the rue de Vaugirard, like the somewhat distant, noble and chivalrous elder he was. He was a candidate for membership of the Académie française and was extremely conscious of it.

Eugène's illness, by detaining the general in Paris, had brought about a rapprochement between Victor and his father which was not merely a family reconciliation, but one between two minds. The severe father in his hey-day had provoked antagonism; the father in retirement, leaning upon his already famous son, inspired indulgence, filial piety, and pride, too, in his past exploits, which Adèle and Victor loved to hear him recount.

Through his father, whom he now knew and loved better, he also drew closer to the Emperor. Living, Napoleon had been the 'tyrant' his mother hated. After the tragedy of St Helena he had become a persecuted hero, and deep in his heart Hugo felt that it was a finer thing for a French poet to sing of 'all the men of Friedland and the men of Rivoli' than to write odes on the trivial pursuits of the royal family.

From 1826 to 1829 Hugo worked a great deal, learned a great deal, and discovered a great deal. In tracing the vast strides which he was making at this time in his art, it would be a mistake to go by publication dates: *Odes et Ballades* (end of 1826), *Cromwell* (1827), *Les Orientales* (1829). He sometimes held back a manuscript for two or three years. *Les Orientales* contains poems written in 1826; the wonderful 'Madman's Song' from *Cromwell* already appears as an epigraph in *Odes et Ballades*.

Frontispiece to the 1860 edition of *Les Orientales*

'The Dream', a pen-and-ink drawing by Victor Hugo

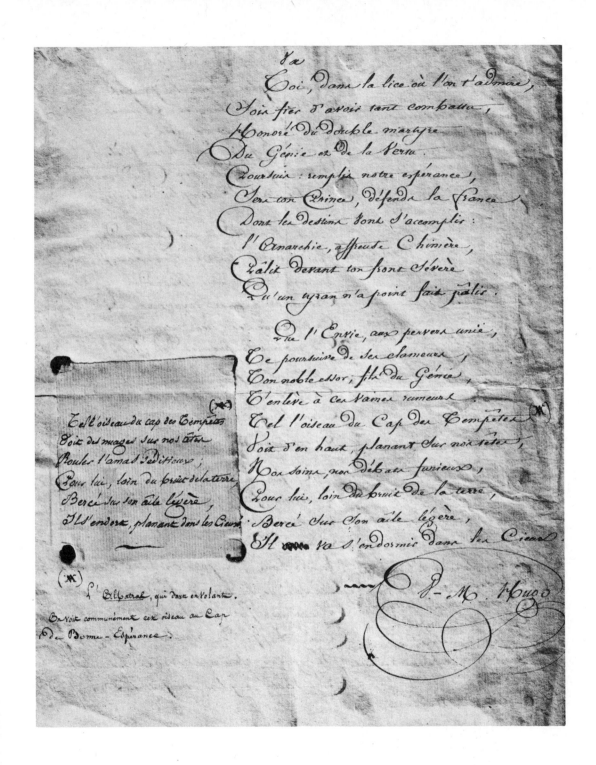

Manuscript page from *Odes et Ballades*

Le Globe, an intelligent and serious journal, had until then been rather unfavourable to Victor Hugo. It was a liberal publication, international in its culture, and it had been annoyed and sometimes angered by *La Muse française* and by the Catholicism of the circle associated with it. However, the editor, Paul-François Dubois, an authoritarian, irascible professor and journalist, confessed himself charmed when he visited the young household of 'the angelic Victor', as Sophie Gay put it.

'Odes et Ballades'

On the publication of *Odes et Ballades* Dubois, who remembered with affection the 'Holy Family' of the rue de Vaugirard, sent the volume to one of his old pupils of the Collège Bourbon, Charles Augustin Sainte-Beuve, who now worked as a critic for *Le Globe*. The critic was even younger than the poet – two years younger – but he had an extensive cultural background, an eye and an ear for subtle distinctions, and one of the most penetrating minds of his time. Delicacy of taste and sureness of judgment were his natural gifts. A vestigial Christian faith struggled within him against a realistic and sceptical spirit, born of his scientific studies. Lyrical and positive in his outlook, he aspired only to one kind of happiness, that of love; and felt keenly his incapacity for inspiring it. The inner meaning interested him more than the picturesqueness of a phrase. He wrote expressing his admiration for 'the fiery style, glittering with images and bounding with harmonies' but what he praised above all in *Odes et Ballades* were the few poems which exceeding mere technical virtuosity, Victor Hugo had wrung from the depths of his soul for the woman he loved.

One can imagine the joy of the young couple as they read, on 2 January 1827, in an habitually severe journal, these praises for the poems dearest to their hearts. Never mind the reservations, the tone of the article was friendly and even respectful. Goethe, who read it, was not mistaken. On 4 January he said to Eckermann: 'Victor Hugo is a really talented writer and German literature has had some influence on him. He was unfortunately belittled during his poetic apprenticeship by the pedantic Classicists, but there he is now with *Le Globe* on his side; so he has won. . . .' Genius is capable of recognizing genius.

The *Globe* article was signed S.B. Victor wrote to Dubois asking him who S.B. was. When Dubois replied: 'He lives close to you, at 94 rue de Vaugirard', Hugo went and rang his neighbour's bell. Sainte-Beuve was out, but the next day he came to the Hugos. They saw a shy young man, frail and awkwardly built, inclined to stammer, and with a long nose. His reddish hair and his round head, too large for his body, were not attractive.

Cromwell

For a year now Victor Hugo had been working on a drama, *Cromwell*. He had always been attracted to the theatre, and had been writing plays since childhood. He had read all he could find about the life of Oliver Cromwell – nearly a hundred volumes. Then, in 1826, he had started work. When Taylor, a friend of de Vigny's who had been raised to the peerage by Charles X, and had become the Commissaire Royale at the Comédie-Française asked him why

Portrait of Talma, the famous actor, by Riesener

Sainte-Beuve at the time of his friendship with Victor Hugo

he never wrote for the theatre, Hugo mentioned his *Cromwell*. Taylor invited him to dinner with Talma, and the poet explained to him what he wanted to do: substitute drama for tragedy and Shakespeare for Racine; introduce a style with universal appeal, a style that would include both heroic and farcical elements; abolish declamatory speeches and lines written for the sake of mere effect. 'O yes!' said Talma, 'No purple passages!'

But Talma died that same year; the play had grown too long; it seemed as if it would never be performed – or at least not in the foreseeable future. Victor Hugo decided to read *Cromwell* to his friends. Readings were the fashion then. On the following day Sainte-Beuve wrote Hugo a very interesting and important letter.

In it, the difference in their temperaments began to be apparent. Hugo, with his vigour, found it impossible, and unnecessary, to renounce the heights; Sainte-Beuve, delicate and fragile by temperament, could breathe only on 'the gentler slopes'. He understood Romanticism as he understood all things; but to his way of thinking the great drama was marred by 'burlesque comedy'. Hugo, the born poet, valued ideas suggested by rhyme, as Michelangelo valued forms suggested by blocks of marble; Sainte-Beuve, the prose writer, believed in the necessity of logical links between ideas. In fact his verses never attained the controlled ecstasy of real poetry. Hugo, more versatile, knew how to bow, when he wished to, to the demands of prose. The preface to *Cromwell* proves this.

It was written after the play and was received, especially by younger people, with unprecedented enthusiasm. For Hugo it constituted a commitment at last. Plagued by the nagging, stupid Classicists, he now assumed the leadership of the rebels.

Victor Hugo's house in the rue Notre-Dame-des-Champs ▶

Caricature of Paul
Foucher, Victor Hugo's
brother-in-law

Birth of Charles   If ever Hugo seemed a happy man it was in 1827 and 1828. A son, Charles, had been born to him in 1826. The first floor in the rue de Vaugirard became too small, so he rented a whole house at 11 rue Notre-Dame-des-Champs, 'a real poet's retreat, hidden away at the bottom of a shady avenue'. Behind it was a romantic garden, with a miniature lake and a rustic bridge. Sainte-Beuve, who could now no longer do without the Hugos, came to live close by at No. 19, in a flat which he shared with his mother. Everyone sees nature in terms of his own temperament. Hugo dearly loved the popular Vaugirard quarter, with its songs, its cries, its shameless kisses. The refined Sainte-Beuve sighed: 'Oh how sad the plain is around the boulevard.' So it was not often in his company that Victor Hugo set off on foot every evening, when his eyes were tired from work, towards the village of Plaisance and the setting sun.

He was surrounded by a little group of 'courtiers'. There was his brother Abel, his brother-in-law Paul Foucher, and a whole troop of artists and poets. They were recruited in quick succession. Hugo, among his other gifts, had that of attracting young men. Pavie put Victor Hugo in touch with the sculptor David d'Angers, who was already well known, and who favoured the idea of a living, modern art. Painters and lithographers had already attached themselves to Hugo's circle: Achille and Eugène Devéria, two proud, handsome young men who shared a studio with Louis Boulanger, were among them. By chance they too lived in the rue Notre-Dame-des-Champs.

On summer evenings they went out in a crowd; they went to eat pastries at the Moulin de Beurre, then they dined at some suburban eating-place on wooden tables, and sang and argued.

Portrait of the painter Eugène Devéria
by Achille Devéria

Portrait of the
sculptor David d'Angers

Often, too, he would repeat to them poems from *Les Orientales*. What gave him this idea of portraying a conventional East? It was the fashion. Greece was struggling for her freedom; Byron had just sacrificed his life for her. Liberal minds the world over defended her, and Hugo's artist friends were liberals. Delphine Gay, Lamartine, Casimir Delavigne, all of them wrote philhellenic poems. With *Les Orientales*, Hugo 'created the unity of the Romantic movement'.

A notebook, 'Dramas to be written', contained plots which would later become, or which had already become, *Marion Delorme, Les Jumeaux, Lucrèce Borgia*; as well as others which were never carried out: *Louis XI, La Mort du duc d'Enghien, Néron*. At the bottom of one page, filled with titles, there is this note: 'When all this is done, I shall see.' Strength like Hugo's creates tremendous self-confidence. There is no doubt about this. His nature was more imperial than royal. Like the youthful Bonaparte, he dominated not by virtue of his birth, not by divine right, but by right of conquest and his own genius; his war-cry was: 'The future, the future, the future is mine!' At that time he little suspected that his character was to be given new depths by the pain caused him by his silent young wife, whom he had made part of his life, and by that red-haired friend with the unpleasant face who said such clever and useful things to him about his work. Even while he was enjoying his triumphs in apparently perfect security, he was on the brink of a catastrophe.

◀ Portrait of
Achille Devéria

Frontispiece to *Bug-Jargal*,
designed by Devéria

Like many people whose youth has been hard, Hugo at twenty-seven was beginning to live; his desire for happiness was as yet unsatisfied, and he took extraordinary pleasure in his success. Probably he was going through his own internal drama at that time: there is no changing sides without violence and injury to oneself. Besides, on a different level, the young husband was not without temptations among his painter friends and their models. The morality of the Vaugirard was not that of the rue du Cherche-Midi.

Adèle, almost always exhausted by pregnancy or nursing a child, was far from sharing the sensual ardours of this 'drunken wine-harvester'. Perhaps he did, in spite of himself, think about other women.

In his poetry of 1829 one can observe the echo of the general's sanguine sensuality. Licentiousness crept into the conversation of the chaste poet of the *Odes*. In *Les Orientales*, side by side with the muse of the *Premier Soupir* shines 'a dazzling Peri lovelier each day'.

Alfred de Vigny

A play-reading in the
green-room of the Comédie-Française

The square in front of Notre-Dame

For the original edition of *Les Orientales*, published by Bossange, he obtained three thousand six hundred francs; from Gosselin, another publisher, seven thousand two hundred francs; for a duodecimo edition of *Les Orientales*, *Bug-Jargal*, *Le Dernier Jour d'un Condamné*, and a novel as yet unwritten, *Notre-Dame de Paris*.

Victor Hugo and Sainte-Beuve

Hugo, a master musician of the language, did not pay enough attention to meaning; Sainte-Beuve, who became a poet because he was first a sensitive man, failed in his poetry because it was awkward and weak in form.

He portrayed himself in all his desolation in an anonymous work, *Vie, Pensées et Poésies de Joseph Delorme*. Joseph Delorme wanted to become a great poet but lacked inspiration. 'What painful tremors he felt at each new triumph of his young contemporaries!' Joseph Delorme had no teacher, no friends, no religion. 'His soul offered nothing but an inconceivable chaos of monstrous imaginings. Great but aborted thoughts, wise foresight followed by crazy action, pious urges in the wake of blasphemies, moved confusedly against a background of despair. . . .' He said that he was 'sick and devoured by never having loved'.

At the end of 1828 Sainte-Beuve had shown Hugo these 'wretched pages' and asked him whether it would be too unsuitable and absurd to deliver to the public gaze this 'laying-bare of the soul'. Hugo had replied with a warmly worded note. It was a happy day for Sainte-Beuve. For a moment he believed himself to be a great poet. In January 1829 *Les Orientales* appeared, in March 1829 *Joseph Delorme*. *Les Orientales* attracted more attention, but their diligent author carefully studied the lessons of *Joseph Delorme*, and drew from it the idea of an intimate and personal kind of poetry.

His friend's successes inspired Sainte-Beuve at that time more with humility than with jealousy. In his writings he became the champion of Hugo's Romanticism and made up for the weakness of his convictions by the warmth of his tone, for he had never really been a Romantic.

The year 1829 was for Victor Hugo, always an indefatigable worker, one of the most laborious years of all. He had begun *Notre-Dame de Paris* and he was writing numerous poems. Above all he wished to conquer the stage. *Cromwell* had not been produced so he decided to try another tack. *Marion Delorme* (original title: *Un Duel sous Richelieu*) was the result. It was set in the reign of Louis XIII, and was the fairly commonplace story of a courtesan purified by her love for a chaste young man of strict morals.

On 14 July the Théatre-Français acclaimed the play. Three days later, Vigny read his *More de Venise* before the same men of letters. Their welcome was no less warm than it had been for *Marion Delorme*. The censorship, powerful at that time, authorized the *More* and banned *Marion*. But because Hugo had always, as a writer, been friendly towards the monarchy, steps were taken to pacify him by means of favours, and a further pension of two thousand francs was offered to him. He refused it in a very dignified letter.

Immediately Hugo began to write another play, *Hernani*. Its subject was reminiscent of *Marion Delorme*. Its motto *Tres para una*, three men striving for one woman. The first of them, young, ardent, and an outlaw, as was proper, was Hernani. The second, a pitiless old man, Don Ruy Gomez de Silva. The third, the King and Emperor Charles V. Its sources are obscure. Certainly among them were the *Romancero*, Corneille, and some Spanish tragedies. Equally certainly the poet used his own *Lettres à la Fiancée* for many of the love themes. *Hernani* was the drama which he himself had experienced with Adèle.

The play was written with unbelievable rapidity. It was begun on 29 August, finished on 25 September and read to Hugo's friends on the 30th. On 5 October it was shown to the Théâtre-Français and was received with acclamation. The censorship, not without some resistance, granted permission for it to be performed.

During the whole of 1829 Hugo worked from morning till night, and sometimes from night until morning; either he was writing, or had to visit the theatre or his publishers, or he was exploring the old part of Paris around Notre-Dame, or composing poems as he walked in the Jardin du Luxembourg.

Théophile Gautier

Birth of
François-Victor

Sainte-Beuve had formed the pleasant custom of visiting the house in the rue Notre-Dame-des-Champs every afternoon, and often twice a day. He would now find Mme Hugo alone by the rustic bridge in the garden. The birth and the nursing of François-Victor had plunged her into the daydreaming which, with so many women, accompanies this condition. Alone with her, Sainte-Beuve discovered that when her illustrious husband was away she slipped into confidences. Why was she weeping? Because all women weep; because compassion is sweet; because sometimes it weighed upon her to be married to a man of genius; because this illustrious husband was a powerful and insatiable lover; because she had already had four children; because she was afraid to have more; because she felt somehow oppressed. Sainte-Beuve refrained from uttering imprudent words, and sang Victor's praises, but confessed himself united to his beautiful interlocutor 'by the brotherhood of suffering' and allowed himself to be softly 'led by her towards the Lord'.

New Year's Day 1830 put an end, alas, to these celestial, fleeting moments. During January the Hugo household was in tumult. The Comédie-Française was rehearsing *Hernani*, and the rehearsals were nothing but a long series of battles between its author and its interpreters.

The Battle of
Hernani

Victor Hugo, absorbed in rehearsals, hardly lived at home any longer. He, who had prided himself on behaving like a model husband and father, no longer belonged to his own family. *Hernani* must succeed, whatever the cost, because legal proceedings had swallowed up their reserves. Adèle, whose purse was empty, stood by her husband and gave herself up completely to this rescue operation.

And now Sainte-Beuve, arriving for his daily visit, would find Mme Hugo surrounded by long-haired young men, all of them bent over a seating plan of the theatre. On the day of the first night he went with Hugo, eight hours before the curtain rose, to watch the arrival of the faithful in the still darkened auditorium. The young Théophile Gautier, who commanded a whole troop of red tickets, was wearing his famous pink doublet, very pale duck-egg green trousers, and a coat with a black velvet collar. The purpose of this sartorial

The Battle of *Hernani*

Three drawings by
Mme Victor Hugo
left Charles Hugo
right Adèle Hugo
far right François-Victor

eccentricity was to exasperate the Philistines. People in the boxes pointed out to each other the extraordinary hair styles of the modern school.

As the final ovation broke out 'the whole auditorium turned to gaze at the woman whose enchanting face was still pale with the preoccupation of the morning and the evening's excitement. The author's triumph was reflected in the face of that most cherished part of himself.'

Receipts exceeded all expectations. *Hernani* refloated the young household. Thousand-franc notes, hitherto so rare in that house, now piled up in Adèle's drawer. Victor, triumphant, was trying to get used to being adored.

Sainte-Beuve raged inwardly. He had just learnt that the Hugos were to move in May to the only house in the new rue Jean-Goujon. The landlord in the rue Notre-Dame-des-Champs, alarmed by the long-haired, bohemian art students of *Hernani*, had given them notice; but the Comte de Mortemart leased to them the second floor of the large house he had just had built. Their new affluence meant that they could now afford the Champs-Élysées. Adèle was expecting her fifth child, and Hugo himself was not sorry to be separated from Sainte-Beuve. The daily visits came to an end. And besides, could they have gone on? The mixture of love and hate which Joseph Delorme felt for Hugo was becoming stifling. He now knew that his feeling for Adèle was one not of friendship but of love. Adèle wept a great deal, and her husband observed it with distress.

On 25 July 1830 all Paris was indignant at Polignac's insane edicts against civil liberties. On the 27th, barricades went up. On the 28th it was 90°F.

in the shade. The Champs-Élysées, a dreary, flat area usually left to small-holders, was covered with troops. In this far-off quarter people were isolated and no news was forthcoming. Bullets whined in the garden. Adèle, the night before, had brought into the world a second Adèle, fat and plump-cheeked. In the distance cannon-fire could be heard. On the 29th a tri-colour flag flew over the Tuileries. What next? A Republic? La Fayette, who might have become its president, feared responsibility as much as he loved popularity. He placed the republican flag in the hands of the Duc d'Orléans. There was no longer a King of France; there was only a King of the French. Victor Hugo accepted the new régime immediately. Since the banning of *Marion Delorme* he had been out of favour at the palace, but he judged France to be not yet ready for a republic.

Birth of Adèle

His 'Ode to Young France' was superior, from a literary point of view, to his legitimist odes of former days, which is an indication of his sincerity. He wished this poem to appear in *Le Globe*, a liberal paper. Sainte-Beuve, who had returned from Normandy, arranged this transfer of allegiance. Hugo went to see him at the printing works of the paper to ask him to stand godfather to his daughter. Sainte-Beuve hesitated, then accepted when he was assured that Adèle wished it.

All was going well for Hugo. He was a member of the National Guard, in the Battalion of the 1st Legion, and secretary of the disciplinary committee, a post which carried no guard duties. His play was being performed, his loyalty was accepted. He could at last turn to the writing of *Notre-Dame de Paris*. The task was urgent. Gosselin, who had published *Les Orientales*, had a contract. Victor

Hugo, recollects a witness, 'bought himself a bottle of ink and a heavy knitted garment of grey wool which enveloped him from his neck to his feet, locked up his clothes to avoid the temptation of going out, and imprisoned himself with his book.'

'Notre-Dame de Paris'

At the beginning of January 1831, Hugo finished *Notre-Dame de Paris*. He had written this novel in six months, which was within the longest period stipulated by Gosselin. In fact, it had only been a question of writing and composing; the material had been gathered together over three years. The archdeacon, Claude Frollo, is a monster; Quasimodo is one of those hideous huge-headed dwarfs that Hugo's imagination teemed with; Esmeralda is a graceful vision rather than a woman.

Nevertheless, these characters were to live in the minds of men of all countries and nationalities. The reason is that they possessed the elemental grandeur of epic myth as well as the more inward truth which they derived from their hidden connexion with the author's fantasies. Capable of love or hatred towards inanimate objects, he could give an extraordinary living quality to a cathedral, a town, or a gibbet. His book was to have a profound influence on French architecture. Buildings dating from before the Renaissance, hitherto considered barbarous, were now to be venerated as if they had been Bibles written in stone. A committee for the preservation of historic monuments was created. Hugo (himself instructed by Nodier) had, in 1831, brought about a revolution in taste.

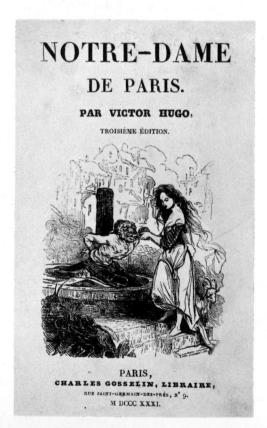

Cover designed by Tony Johannot for the 1831 edition of *Notre-Dame de Paris*

Characters from *Notre-Dame de Paris*:
the hunchback Quasimodo,
Esmeralda and her goat,
and Gringoire

A husband in his glory is not necessarily a lovable person. Quite the contrary. As a mother gives herself to her child, the poet gives himself to his work. He becomes exacting, dominating, authoritarian. Adèle, as she had foreseen ever since their betrothal, found in Victor a tyrannical lord and master; she felt homesick for her timid and submissive confidant. It is certain that she saw Sainte-Beuve again, secretly; that she saw him alone; that she imprudently reported to him her husband's words; and that the clandestine pair even got into the habit, when out of reach of the 'Cyclops', of criticizing him without mercy.

This transition from marital fidelity to betrayal of heart and mind took several months to accomplish. In April 1831 Adèle pressed the two men for a reconciliation. The fact that these quarrels made her ill still touched them both. Sainte-Beuve wrote to Hugo: 'May I come and shake you by the hand?' Hugo replied: 'You'll come and dine with us one of these days, won't you?' By this

Illustration from the 1831 edition of *Les Feuilles d'Automne*

time Sainte-Beuve had read *Notre-Dame de Paris*. In spite of a sprinkling of praise he did not like the book enough to write an article about it. Hugo knew this, and the invitation was therefore a disinterested one. This return to half-intimacy was not a happy one. There was a lack of confidence on both sides. Hugo kept watch on his wife and his friend when they were together. Alone with Adèle, he made scenes. At first she would try to pacify him with sweetness, then she would lose patience: 'Is it my fault if I love you less than you torment me?' Then he would throw himself at her feet; and afterwards write to her: 'Forgive me.' Sainte-Beuve now addressed to the loved one verses whose familiarity strengthened the intimacy; he considered these amorous elegies to be his finest productions. She replied with letters in which she called Sainte-Beuve 'My dear angel . . . Beloved treasure. . . .' Poor Adèle! The little Foucher girl, the precise little clerk's daughter, was fitted neither for romantic drama nor for romantic comedy. She was an introvert, a perfect mother, full of affection. Her senses remained calm and undisturbed. She would have liked to keep her husband and her friend too; both of them in an equal state of chastity.

Hugo had staked his whole existence on this love. He had struggled for three years to win his wife, and he had lived for eight years in the belief that he was for her the object of a religious devotion. He had dreamed of building the perfect relationship, at once romantic, chivalrous, sensual and pure. Absorbed in his work and his battles, he had not suspected the presence of this disappointed heart beside him. His awakening was terrible. But a poet can by a strange transmutation turn his pain into song. In November 1831 *Les Feuilles d'Automne* appeared.

'*Les Feuilles d'Automne*'

This collection was far superior to *Odes et Ballades* and *Les Orientales*. Sainte-Beuve was a poor guest but a good master. By passing through the crucible of the magician, the intimate poetry of Joseph Delorme had achieved formal perfection without losing its 'indefinable plaintiveness'.

But they were the leaves of a premature autumn. The soul has lived, and by living changed:

A scene from
Le Roi s'amuse

By dint of walking man wanders from his path, and the mind is invaded by doubt.
Everything leaves something on the hedge by the roadside.
Sheep their wool, man his virtue.

No one has spoken better than Sainte-Beuve of the moving beauty and the painful scepticism of these poems.

1832: Victor Hugo was only thirty, but he was marked by struggle and sorrow. His face and figure had coarsened. One saw no more the angelic charm of his eighteenth year, or the conquering look of his first days of marriage. His authority was more that of the emperor than of the knight. Hugo would write one day that there were in him four beings: Olympio, the lyric poet; Hernani, the lover; Maglia, the jester; and Hierro, the warrior. It is true that he liked fighting, but he still needed to feel that he had support. Friends who could be relied upon were few.

The house in the place Royale (now place des Vosges) to which the Hugos moved in October 1832

Victor Hugo aged thirty

The case of Sainte-Beuve was unusual. In terms of literature, he remained officially an ally, not without reservations; in terms of human relationships he was acting as a traitor, and excusing his conduct by his passion. He no longer visited the Hugos, but continued to inquire for news of the 'dear family', as for instance in the spring of 1832, when little Charlot had, or was believed to have, cholera. But he was still meeting Adèle in secret.

In October 1832 the Hugos moved house again. In July they had rented a large apartment at 6 place Royale, on the first floor of the Hôtel de Guéménée, a stately mansion built in about 1604, and facing one of the most beautiful squares in Paris: green foliage, red bricks, gabled slate roofs; the present place des Vosges.

If the square and the buildings were lordly, the area in which they found themselves was popular enough: 'We, the poor workmen of the Faubourg Saint-Antoine', Hugo liked to say. Success had not given him a very good conscience. In 1828 he had published *Le Dernier Jour d'Un Condamné*: in 1832 it was *Claude Gueux*. The theme was again that of injustice and suffering. Again there were the same attacks on a society whose laws benefited the rich and powerful.

The shortest road to a literary fortune seemed, at that time, to be the theatre. *The Theatre* Besides, Hugo was aware that the medium could – and should – exert a moral and political influence: 'The theatre is a platform. The theatre is a pulpit.' His favourite subject for drama was still the defence of the outcast against his oppressors.

The first night of *Le Roi s'amuse* took place on 22 November. Although the demagogues and 'Young France' – all Théophile's and all Devéria's men – were at their posts, the auditorium seemed chilly. At the final curtain, the storm was such that the actor Ligier had difficulty in announcing the author's name. The next day the Minister, the Comte d'Argout, banned the play 'in view of the threat it presents to public morality'.

General Hugo's son had never shrunk from a battle. The banning of *Le Roi s'amuse*, far from discouraging him, made him long for immediate revenge. He had another play ready: *Le Souper à Ferrare*, three acts in prose, inspired by his reading of Marchangy's *Gaule poétique*. Hugo's plays were distinctly inferior to his lyric poems. But the stage has its own aesthetic; at that time melodrama had conquered tragedy; and it seemed quite natural to perform *Lucrèce Borgia* in the very theatre in which *La Tour de Nesle* had been produced.

The theatre was the Porte-Saint-Martin, and its director, Harel, had the illustrious actress Mlle George for a mistress. Victor Hugo read his play once to her at her apartment, and then in the green-room of the Porte-Saint-Martin theatre, for Frédérick Lemaître. At this second reading there was present a *Juliette Drouet* young and beautiful actress, Juliette Drouet, who had agreed to play a small part, that of the Princess Negroni. Victor Hugo did not know her, but had caught sight of her one evening at a ball, in May 1832, 'pale, with dark eyes, young, tall, brilliant' and covered with jewels. She was one of the most dazzling beauties in Paris. He had not dared to speak to her. During the reading they became immediately and mutually fascinated. Later Victor wrote in Juliette's notebook: 'The first time your eyes looked into mine, a ray of light passed from your heart into mine like the first rays of dawn into a ruin.' To tell the truth each of them, without knowing it, was in the presence of a being in distress.

For Hugo, after a year of humiliation, this love affair was like a resurrection. The idea of taking a mistress, of spending nights away from home, had at first shocked him, the poet of the hearth and of the family. Then he began to take some pride in it. He spoke to everyone about his conquest, even to Sainte-Beuve, who poked fun at him. The angel of forgiveness was Adèle. To be sure, the angels part came naturally to her. How could she have done anything but forgive? And how, if she were unwilling to be his wife, could she demand his marital faithfulness?

Juliette's history was that she had become a courtesan, in all innocence, and had found it natural, since she encountered only cynicism and brutality among men, to expect at least luxury at the hands of a Prince Demidoff or one of his kind. And now here she was in love with a demanding monster, who despised venality, refused to share her, and had suffered too much from jealousy himself not to insist upon certainty now. Because he loved her with a 'total, deep, burning, inexhaustible and infinite' love, he wanted her to be as pure as she was beautiful.

He for his part was willing to forgive her if she broke with her past. She at last submitted and found herself very badly off.

Victor's seriousness and solemnity, which had irritated Adèle, pleased Juliette; all the more so because they alternated with a kind of student gaiety which she found delightful.

Only one hope now remained for her: a theatrical career. Hugo, after numerous quarrels, had promised Félix Harel a new play for the Porte-Saint-Martin theatre: *Marie Tudor*. He wished to give two almost equal parts in it to Mlle George and Mlle Juliette. Rehearsals were stormy. The day before the first night the producer said to the author: 'Mlle Juliette is impossible. Mlle Ida, Dumas's mistress, knows the part and is ready and willing to play it.' Hugo was too much in love and too fond of justice to give in. The evening began in an atmosphere of gathering storm. The first two acts were uneventful, but whistles greeted Juliette's scenes in the third. Put out by the hostility of company and audience alike, she justified, alas, both fears and criticism. The next day, under pressure from Sainte-Beuve, from Adèle and from the 'old campaigners of *Hernani*', Hugo, angry and hurt, was forced to consent to the replacement of the

Mlle George, the famous actress who had been Napoleon's mistress

Costume worn by Juliette Drouet in the part of the Princess Negroni in *Lucrèce Borgia*

unfortunate Juliette, on the grounds of her indisposition – a genuine one, since she had to take to her bed. The unkindness of the audience's reception had finally destroyed the little dramatic talent poor Juliette had left.

The year 1834 witnessed a complete rupture between Sainte-Beuve and Victor Hugo, not for emotional reasons, but because of divergent literary viewpoints.

For Victor Hugo and Juliette Drouet it was a year of chaos. Peaks of sublimity; abysses of gloom. The only stable feature of the changing climate of the life they shared was their mutual love, corporal and spiritual. She expressed it touchingly: 'If life could buy happiness mine would have been spent long ago. . . .'

But one cannot live on love or intelligence, and she was a poor girl loaded with debts. By August her pack of creditors had found the scent and were baying so loudly that Juliette had at last to confess to her lover the amount she owed. Twenty thousand francs. General Hugo's son, the boy who for so long had earned no more than two sous a day, flew into a terrible rage; he said he would pay it all bit by bit, even if he had to compromise his health and his very existence; but these promises were mingled with the severest reproaches.

Then began the most amazing life of penitence and cloistered renunciation that a woman has ever accepted, outside monastic orders. Juliette, who the day before had been one of the most admired women in Paris, covered in lace and jewels, was now to live only for him, to go out only with him, to give up all her coquetry and all her luxury; in short, to do penance. She agreed, in a mystical intoxication of 'redemption through love'.

In her free time she copied her lover's manuscripts or mended his clothes. That was still pleasant for her. What was painful was that not being able to go out by herself, she had to wait days on end, looking at the blue sky like a bird in a cage. Her only hope of independence, which she persisted in despite her many disappointments, remained the theatre. Victor Hugo had finished a new prose drama, *Angelo, tyran de Padoue*. It was a melodrama in the manner of *Lucrèce Borgia*, but it was well constructed, and the Comédie-Française accepted it enthusiastically.

Now Juliette was a member of the Comédie-Française. Might she not hope for one of the two parts? She guessed that Hugo was reluctant to trust his play to an actress whose talent was in question and who was being hounded by a rival faction, and that he dared not tell her so. She left the Théâtre-Française without ever having played in it. The parts went to Mlle Mars and Mlle Dorval.

Supreme humiliation for the actress, and cause of misgiving for the lover: Marie Dorval's disturbing coquetry and fatal charm were well known. Juliette's unqualified admiration, which was almost religious devotion, had the unfortunate effect of encouraging the poet towards an apotheosis. The Romantics, in order to escape their terrestrial destinies more easily, were then accustomed to creating doubles into whom they could put both their ambitions and their sufferings. Byron had set the example with *Childe Harold*; de Vigny had had his

Victor Hugo with a group of his contemporaries in 1833 ▶

LES ARTISTES

Lith. de Lemercier rue du Four S.G. N°55.

CONTEMPORAINS.

1. Chateaubriand. 3. V. Hugo.
2. C. Delavigne.   4. Béranger.

5. A^{dre} Dumas.   7. de Lamartine.
6. Lemercier.   8. Étienne.

Paris chez Delta rue J. Jacquet N 38.

Léopoldine Hugo aged thirteen

Stello; Musset his *Fortunio* and *Fantasio*; George Sand, *Lélia*; Sainte-Beuve, *Joseph Delorme*; Chateaubriand, *René*; Stendhal, *Julien Sorel*; Goethe, *Wilhelm Meister*; Benjamin Constant, *Adolphe*. Hugo incarnated himself in *Olympio*, 'who', said Maurice Levaillant, 'resembled him like a brother, he was a demigod, born in solitude, caressed in turn by the winds of pride, of nature and of love. . . .' He went, then, through a painful period, in which he knew that he was detested and calumniated. 'Nearly all his old friends', wrote Heinrich Heine, 'have left him; and if truth be told, it is his own fault that they have done so. They have been so wounded by his egoism.'

Passion, in the full and tragic sense of the word, was now to mould a poet infinitely surpassing not only the author of *Odes et Ballades*, but even that of *Les Feuilles d'Automne*. *Les Chants du Crépuscule*, published at the end of October 1835 by Renduel, was a collection of masterpieces. The title gave one to expect a softened light; in fact, after the fireworks of *Les Orientales*, here was a truly admirable combination of simplicity of tone and definition of outline.

It is natural for a young man to write love poems; a poet approaching the prime of life expects something different from himself. Between 1836 and 1840 Victor Hugo became worried about not playing any public role. To sing the woods, the sun and Juliette was good, but could hardly fill the life of a man who wished to be 'guiding spirit'.

Collections dating from this period – *Les Voix intérieurs* (1837), *Les Rayons et les Ombres* (1840)—begin to inquire more deeply into the nature of things. On the mountain peaks, on coastal promontories, the poet leans over the abyss and converses with God.

Juliette Drouet,
in the year
Lucrèce Borgia
was performed

Action, on the other hand, does not require metaphysical certitude. 'This century is large and powerful; a noble instinct leads it on'; and Hugo wanted to be among the men who would mould nations. Chateaubriand, his model, had been a peer of France, an ambassador, and Minister of Foreign Affairs. This was the royal road he meant to follow henceforth. The only thing was, that for a writer to obtain a peerage under Louis-Philippe, he had to be a member of the Académie-Française.

His mistress and his daughter, Juliette and Didine, were both hostile towards the green coat; they had been brought up to loathe fripperies like that and they stuck to their opinions. Juliette feared that the candidature, and the social obligations which it would entail, might draw her lover away from her.

The wedding of Ferdinand Philippe, Duc d'Orléans, and Princess Hélène of Mecklenburg, which took place in 1837 at the Château de Fontainebleau

Frédérick Lemaître in
the fifth act of *Ruy
Blas*, on the occasion
of its first performance

When, in February 1836, the day of the election arrived (it was a question of
replacing Vicomte Laine), she predicted his failure with joy in her heart.

The beaten but undiscouraged candidate returned to daily life. He became
more and more attached to his children. Didine, a charming, sensible, subtle,
discreet girl, remained his favourite and became his confidante.

On Juliette's side all was love, though stormy and handicapped by poverty.
He had installed her in the Marais, at 14 rue Saint-Anastase, within reach of the
place Royale. The walls of the little flat were covered with portraits of, and
drawings by the household deity.

He was not insensible to the pleasure of being thus adored. Not that the
adoration was blind. Juliette had her rancours and jealousies – justifiable ones
too, since there was a concealed staircase at the place Royale which communicated directly with Victor Hugo's writing-room, and Juliette, who had
entered by this way herself, was not ignorant of the fact that other women had
been drawn up it by the charms of the master.

Perhaps Juliette would not have borne it without the travelling; but every
summer those wonderful interludes were hers. One would go (that is to say,
Adèle would go) to Fourqueux or Boulogne-sur-Seine and set up house with
the four children, and then for six weeks the lovers, whose relationship became
for the time being almost marital, would leave for Juliette's native Fougères,
or for Belgium, whose carillons and belfries and ancient houses fascinated
Hugo. She would have been very happy to have gone with him on his pilgrimage to the Metz household near Bièvre, where they had been so happy at
the beginning of their liaison; but he chose to go there without her, in October
1837, to be alone with their memories.

Victor Hugo, de Vigny, Alexandre Dumas and Balzac, as seen by Granville in this caricature of 'The Académie-Française steeplechase'

'*Tristesse d'Olympio*'

The product of those days of wandering and musing in the land of his sweetest adventure, was a poem: *Tristesse d'Olympio*. Why 'sadness' after such joys? Because Romantic writers view with pain the contrast between the eternal beauty of nature and the ephemeral happiness of man.

In 1837 the Duc d'Orléans married Princess Hélène of Mecklenburg. Victor Hugo's relations with the heir to the throne were better than his relations with Louis-Philippe.

When Louis-Philippe gave a banquet in the Hall of Mirrors at Versailles, in honour of his eldest son's marriage, Hugo was invited. He was placed at the Duc d'Aumale's table. The king paid him handsome compliments. The Duchesse d'Orléans, a cultured, intelligent woman with a beautiful open face, told him that she was happy to see him; that she had often spoken of him with M. de Goethe; that she knew his poems by heart, and that she loved above all others the one which began: 'It was a humble church with a low-arching vault. . . .' All this was true. He became the poet of the future Queen of the French; no reception could take place at the Pavillon de Marsan without him. When the Duc d'Orléans expressed his surprise at Hugo's having given up drama, he replied that the theatre no longer existed 'since the Comédie-Française has been consecrated to the dead, and the Porte-Saint-Martin given over

Hugo being received by the Académie Française. Watercolour by Hermann Vogel ▶

to animals.' The Prince, through M. Guizot, offered the author the extraordinary privilege of founding a new theatre. It was to be known as the Renaissance, as Dumas and Hugo confided to Anténor Joly, the newspaper editor. For the inauguration Hugo was expected to supply a play in verse.

Ruy Blas   Where did the subject matter of *Ruy Blas* come from? In fact its sources are not important. The drama, a mixture of poetry, of farce, of fantasy and of politics, is essentially Hugoesque.

The play, completed in three months, was the best he had yet written. The heroic verse rang out like that of the classics of the Great Age; the rhyme, rich and resonant, punctuated speeches of which at least one (in Act III) is a masterpiece of poetry and history. Frédérick Lemaître played Ruy Blas.

Hugo still longed to enter the Académie-Française, and he was accustomed to getting what he wanted. He beat Ancelot, 'a third-rate playwright', on 7

Entry into the   January 1841, by seventeen votes to fifteen. Chateaubriand, Lamartine, Ville-
Académie Française   main, Nodier, Cousin and Mignet voted for him, as did political figures such as Thiers, Molé, Salvandy, Royer-Collard. This, he thought, was a pointer, perhaps an invitation. Guizot, who was in favour of Hugo, arrived late and could not vote. Juliette had been hostile to this fifth candidature.

Hugo's entrance was imperial. His smooth brown hair, carefully combed, revealed the monumental forehead, and fell in ringlets on the green embroidered collar. His dark eyes, somewhat deep-set and small, shone with

Caricature of Victor
Hugo after the failure
of *Les Burgraves*

'Burg à la Croix', an impression by Victor Hugo

suppressed happiness. His first smile was for Juliette who, seeing him come in looking so pale and moved, believed she was going to faint.

The ties of the flesh were weaker than they had been at first, but Juliette was still everything that Adèle had been unable or unwilling to become; the gallant traveller, the diligent copyist, the sweet singer of praises, the incarnation of poetry. It was to her, still, that his hymns of thanksgiving were addressed.

Juliette had been his travelling companion on three journeys (in 1838, 1839 and 1840) to the Rhine, that vast, fantastic haunt of the antiquary and the dreamer. Strange, almost magical, was the attraction the great river, with its burden of legend, held for Hugo. Night after night as a child at the Feuillantines he had gazed at the picture above his bed of an old ruined tower, the source, in his daydreams and his drawings, of so many sombre images. Even if he knew little of German literature, he had nevertheless, like his friends Nerval and Gautier, read Hoffman's beautiful *Tales*. Above all he believed that he could see, in the problem of Franco-German relations, the means for a writer to make himself useful and to gain access to public affairs. Therefore, in 1841, he added a political conclusion to the legends, pictures and musings on the past which went into *Le Rhin*.

The poet had attempted to discover in living impressions the answer to an historical question. 'In the simplicity of the old towns of the Palatine he sought to discover the secrets of the past and to pierce the veil of the future. . . .'

Léopoldine Hugo and Charles Vacquerie at the time of their marriage

He saw the Rhine as terrible, epic, 'Aeschylean'. The drawings, very fine ones, with which he returned all glowed with this tragic, supernatural, violent and nightmarish light, which emanated rather from Hugo's own character than from the Rhineland itself. More and more, he began to use two styles. One of them, in Sainte-Beuve's words, never cast off 'its ostentation and its pomposity', whereas the other (*Choses vues*) remained that of the consummate reporter. Balzac, who was by no means always indulgent towards Hugo, judged *Le Rhin* to be 'a masterpiece'.

'*Les Burgraves*'

January 1843: Juliette was disturbed to find her 'dear little man' in a state of gloom, even though the new year had come in full of hope. For the first time in five years Hugo was about to have a new play produced: *Les Burgraves*. His daughter Léopoldine had become engaged to a young man whom the family liked very much: Charles Vacquerie. The wedding was arranged to take place in February; *Les Burgraves* would open in March, at the Comédie-Française. In the summer Juliette and Victor were to travel in Spain. What could be more delightful?

On 15 February 1843 the marriage was solemnized, privately and without being announced to Victor Hugo's friends. Juliette, who could not with propriety be present at the ceremony, stayed away from the church but begged Didine to send her a little momento. It would serve as a link between the two beings who loved Hugo most, his daughter and his mistress. The poet was sad to see the departure of his eldest daughter, his favourite, who had been so precociously serious, and so close to him. 'Don't worry about your Didine,' wrote Juliette, 'she will be the happiest of women. . . .' The truth was that everything seemed to proclaim this, but it was true also that Hugo was ill-at-ease and full of vague fears. Léopoldine was to go and live at Le Havre, and it was two days by coach, or by water, from Le Havre to Paris at that time.

Letters arrived, radiant with happiness. The rehearsals for *Les Burgraves* began and rescued Hugo from his strange forebodings. He placed great hopes in this play. He had endeavoured to give it epic stature. It was on his journeys on the Rhine and his visits by day and by night to the ruined castles, pierced by trees and overgrown with brambles, that he had had the vision of the titanic struggle of the Burgraves against the Emperor – 'the formidable barons of the Rhine, in their embattled lairs and served by kneeling officers. . . . Men of prey who have in them something of the owl as well as of the eagle' – and had thought of making a play of it. And then to the struggle of the Burgraves had been added another theme that always haunted Hugo: that of enmity between brothers. The Comédie-Française had been enthusiastic. But the public was gradually moving away from Romantic drama. For several seasons now Rachel, a young actress of outstanding ability, had been restoring the Classical tragedy to favour. The public had become tired of 'that which of all things palls fastest – novelty'.

The first night was quiet, the auditorium being packed with well-wishers. In spite of some fine lines, the play appeared solemn and tedious. After the fifth, each performance was stormy. Hugo kept up an appearance of serenity, but so much hatred, the penalty for so much success, seriously upset him. After thirty-three performances the play was taken off, and Hugo ceased to write for the theatre. 7 March 1843 had been, in the words of Levaillant, 'the Waterloo of Romantic drama'.

Despite Adèle's opposition, Juliette Drouet's 'poor little annual pleasure' took place in the summer. This year it took the form of a trip to the southwest of France and to Spain, which must have revived childhood memories for Victor Hugo, and this cured the melancholy which in Paris had seemed to surround him since February. Léopoldine, three months pregnant and unreasonably anxious, had insisted that her father should not go away. On Tuesday 9 July he went to Normandy to bid her *au revoir*, and afterwards wrote: 'If you only knew, my daughter, how childish I am when I think of you! My eyes fill with tears: I never want to leave you . . . that day at Le Havre is a ray of light among my thoughts; I shall never forget it while I live. . . .'

All the same, the journey tempted him. He went as far as Pamplona, and then returned by way of the Pyrenees, Auch, Agen, Périgueux and Angoulême. On

Villequier

the Île d'Oléron, on 8 September, Juliette observed that he was bowed down with melancholy. The next day, fleeing the island, they arrived in Rochefort, on their way home. Hugo wanted to go to Le Havre to see the young Vacqueries. At the village of Soubise, Juliette suggested stopping at a café to drink a bottle of beer and read the papers which they had not seen for several days. *Juliette Drouet's Diary*, 9 September 1843: 'Under a table opposite us there were several papers. Toto took one at random and I picked up *Le Charivari*. I had hardly had time to read the headline when my poor loved one suddenly leaned towards me and said in a stifled voice, showing me the paper he was holding: "How horrible!" I looked up at him. Never, as long as I live, shall I forget the nameless despair which came over his noble features.'

The story in *Le Siècle* was of a frightful accident which had happened on Monday 4 September at Villequier. Léopoldine and her husband had left Le Havre two days before, to spend the week-end at Villequier. There they had

The cemetery at Villequier where Charles and Léopoldine are buried

Manuscript of Victor Hugo's poem *À Villequier*

Mme Biard
(born Léonie d'Aunet)

met their uncle Pierre Vacquerie, a former ship's captain, and his son Arthus, a young boy of twelve. 'On Sunday afternoon a racing dinghy, which Charles had had brought from Le Havre, arrived there. It was a brain-child of his uncle's, who had had it built to his own design in a naval dockyard. Charles had won a first prize with it at the Honfleur regatta. . . . He intended to try it out next morning by sailing to Caudebec to see Bazire, his solicitor, who was expecting him. . . .' Monday morning was fine; not a breath of wind, not a ripple, only a morning haze. It had been arranged, the day before, that Léopoldine would go with her husband, her uncle and her cousin. 'Elements and objects

– everything betrayed its promise. Happiness, misfortune; the game was played and lost. Of the passengers only Charles, an excellent swimmer, struggled round the overturned hull, trying to save his wife. She clung fast to the boat. He exhausted himself in vain. Then, very simply, he, who had never left her, allowed himself to sink, in order to be with her once again . . .!'

Victor Hugo was shattered by his daughter's death; he was still acutely depressed in December. Sensuality is a violent condition. In extreme confusion of mind, it is natural that a man should seek forgetfulness in variegated and violent sensations. Victor Hugo in 1843, sad to the point of illness, was forced to seek refuge in passion. With Juliette? No. Juliette was not equal to his needs. Cloistered for ten years, the poor girl had faded. At thirty her hair had begun to go grey. She still had her fine eyes and her noble tenderness of manner, but she was no longer 'the beauty that cannot be painted'. At times she depressed him. What, for all her enchanting wit, had she to say? Apart from her month's travelling once a year she saw nothing and no one. Her innumerable letters were nothing but long recitals, mixtures of praises and complaints.

At the beginning of 1844 the reigning mistress, unknown to Juliette, was a *Léonie d'Aunet* young blonde with sad eyes, often lowered, a girl whose dove-like shyness was occasionally belied by a swift, malicious smile. She called herself Léonie d'Aunet. Her family was obscure but genuinely aristocratic. She had been brought up, as a young girl, in society, and had then run away to live with a painter, François-Thérèse-Auguste Biard, in his studio in the place Vendôme.

In 1840, when his companion was six months pregnant, the painter had married her. The couple bought 'a house, a garden, a paddock, a stretch of water and a boat' on the banks of the Seine, near Samois, where they entertained a great many artists.

In 1844, overwhelmed by the Villequier tragedy, Hugo had to make an effort to free himself from his misery. He wanted to deaden all feeling with hard work, with public life (he was active at the Académie and at Court) and certainly also with new love affairs. It is painful to see the same words and feelings going back to work again under a different dispensation. The truth is that a man cannot change completely; the part of the beloved never changes, and Hugo did no more than offer it to a younger actress who was better equipped to play it.

In 1845 Hugo's enemies were under the impression that he was hardly writing. They were mistaken. He was composing fine poems about his daughter and madrigals for Léonie. He was working on a novel, *Les Misères*. But the apparent frivolity of his existence encouraged their malignant hopes. In the Académie he was serious; his face set and his brow furrowed; occasionally rebellious but always dignified.

Victor Hugo no sooner wore the green coat of the Académie than he began to hanker after the golden one of the peerage. Juliette did not want a political career for him: 'To become an Academician, a Peer of France, a Minister – what is all that compared to what God has given to Toto?' . . . Mme Biard, on the other hand, stimulated and encouraged his ambition. Hugo took pains to serve the king; and at the same time he intrigued.

Peer of France   The Duchesse d'Orléans pestered her august father-in-law. Hugo delivered fine speeches at the Académie Française. He brought to bear 'all his heavy artillery', as Sainte-Beuve put it. His tactics secured a victory. An ordinance of 13 April 1845 raised him to the peerage: Vicomte Hugo (Victor Marie).

On 5 July, at the request of Auguste Biard, the Commissary of Police of the Vendôme quarter entered, in the name of the law, and at daybreak, a discreet apartment in the passage Saint-Roch, and surprised there, 'in criminal conversation', Victor Hugo and his mistress. Adultery was at that time severely

Caricature on the subject of Victor Hugo's speech to the Assembly on 11 November 1848

treated and the husband was without pity. Léonie d'Aunet, 'wife of Biard', was arrested and conveyed to the Saint-Lazare prison. Victor Hugo invoked the inviolability of the peerage, and the Commissary, after some hesitation, released him. The affair of the passage Saint-Roch did no permanent damage to his career.

Victor Hugo pursued a policy of silence after this scandal. Not that he ceased to work. He had again taken up *Les Misères*, an old project for which he had entered into a contract with Renduel and Gosselin.

Juliette, without knowing it, reaped the benefit of the incarceration and enforced retreat of Léonie Biard, and enjoyed more often than usual the presence of her lover and master. In 1846 she found herself much closer to him, by reason of a bereavement as terrible as that of Hugo at Villequier. Her daughter Claire Pradier had been unofficially adopted by Hugo, who had paid the child's boarding fees, taught her and loaded her with presents. He was sincerely fond of her. She had grown into a pathetic young girl who was driven by some inner despair into wishing for her own death. When Claire Pradier was buried in the Saint-Mandé cemetery, Vicomte Hugo, peer of France, officiated with her father at her funeral.

After the Biard affair, Hugo felt a wind of icy coldness blowing, and he therefore made a very prudent maiden speech in the House of Peers in 1845. When one is considered disturbing, it is wise to seem dull. His own glory and the death of other men were combining to push him to the forefront. Who in the world of letters was capable of outclassing him? In ten years he had written, starting with *Feuilles d'Automne* and ending with *Les Rayons et les Ombres*, the four finest collections in French poetry; *Les Misérables* promised to be equal to *Notre-Dame de Paris*; and he might yet become a Minister. And still he was not happy. In his distress he sought oblivion. He 'had recourse to the abyss'. Debutantes, adventuresses, chambermaids, courtesans; during the years 1847 to 1850 he seemed to be suffering from a gloomy and almost pathological hunger for new flesh.

On 23 February 1848, on his way to the House of Peers to learn the news, Hugo noticed that the streets were full of soldiers and of workmen in smocks shouting 'Vive la ligne! À bas Guizot!' The soldiers were chatting and joking. In the lobby of the House there were busy, worried-looking groups of men.

Being a courageous man and a passionate observer of mankind who trusted nothing but the evidence of his own eyes, Hugo went and mingled with the crowd in the place de la Concorde. The troops fired on the crowd; some of them were wounded. On 25 February Lamartine told him the provisional government had appointed Victor Hugo mayor of his arrondissement, but that if he would prefer a ministry . . .

When the April elections were held, Hugo, without offering himself as a candidate, issued a 'Letter to the Electors', in which dignity and ambition were decently blended.

VICTOR HUGO

A SES CONCITOYENS.

MES CONCITOYENS,

Je réponds à l'appel des soixante mille Electeurs qui m'ont spontanément honoré de leurs suffrages aux élections de la Seine. Je me présente à votre libre choix.

Dans la situation politique telle qu'elle est, on me demande toute ma pensée. La voici:

Deux Républiques sont possibles.

L'une abattra le drapeau tricolore sous le drapeau rouge, fera des gros sous avec la colonne, jettera bas la statue de Napoléon et dressera la statue de Marat, détruira l'Institut, l'Ecole polytechnique et la Légion-d'Honneur, ajoutera à l'auguste devise : *Liberté, Égalité, Fraternité*, l'option sinistre : *ou la Mort*; fera banqueroute, ruinera les riches sans enrichir les pauvres, anéantira le crédit, qui est la fortune de tous, et le travail, qui est le pain de chacun, abolira la propriété et la famille, promènera des têtes sur des piques, remplira les prisons par le soupçon et les videra par le massacre, mettra l'Europe en feu et la civilisation en cendre, fera de la France la patrie des ténèbres, égorgera la liberté, étouffera les arts, décapitera la pensée, niera Dieu; remettra en mouvement ces deux machines fatales qui ne vont pas l'une sans l'autre, la planche aux assignats et la bascule de la guillotine; en un mot, fera froidement ce que les hommes de 93 ont fait ardemment, et, après l'horrible dans le grand que nos pères ont vu, nous montrera le monstrueux dans le petit.

L'autre sera la sainte communion de tous les Français dès à présent, et de tous les peuples un jour, dans le principe démocratique; fondera une liberté sans usurpations et sans violences, une égalité qui admettra la croissance naturelle de chacun, une fraternité, non de moines dans un couvent, mais d'hommes libres; donnera à tous l'enseignement comme le soleil donne la lumière, gratuitement; introduira la clémence dans la loi pénale et la conciliation dans la loi civile; multipliera les chemins de fer, reboisera une partie du territoire, en défrichera une autre, décuplera la valeur du sol; partira de ce principe qu'il faut que tout homme commence par le travail et finisse par la propriété, assurera en conséquence la propriété comme la représentation du travail accompli et le travail comme l'élément de la propriété future; respectera l'héritage, qui n'est autre chose que la main du père tendue aux enfants à travers le mur du tombeau; combinera pacifiquement, pour résoudre le glorieux problème du bien-être universel, les accroissements continus de l'industrie, de la science, de l'art et de la pensée; poursuivra, sans quitter terre pourtant, et sans sortir du possible et du vrai, la réalisation sereine de tous les grands rêves des sages; bâtira le pouvoir sur la même base que la liberté, c'est-à-dire sur le droit; subordonnera la force à l'intelligence; dissoudra l'émeute et la guerre, ces deux formes de la barbarie; fera de l'ordre la loi des citoyens, et de la paix la loi des nations; vivra et rayonnera, grandira la France, conquerra le monde, sera en un mot le majestueux embrassement du genre humain sous le regard de Dieu satisfait.

De ces deux Républiques, celle-ci s'appelle la civilisation, celle-là s'appelle la terreur. Je suis prêt à dévouer ma vie pour établir l'une et empêcher l'autre.

VICTOR HUGO.

IMPRIMERIE DE JULES-JUTEAU ET Cⁱᵉ, RUE ST-DENIS, 345.

A poster for Victor Hugo who stood as a candidate in the supplementary elections of 4 June 1848

Louis-Napoleon at the barricades, after the *coup d'état* of 2 December 1851

He was not elected, but on 23 April he had the support of sixty thousand votes. After a manifesto of this kind, these votes were a credit to the electorate of Paris. This half-success gained him the support, in the supplementary elections, of the committee of the rue de Poitiers, that is to say, of the conservatives.

Victor Hugo was elected. By which party? He only knew that he was 'for the small people against the great', and for order against anarchy. He himself doubtless felt the weakness of his position, for in July 1848 he determined to equip himself with a different means of influencing public opinion by founding a newspaper, *L'Événement*. He still, at this time, wished it to be an 'organ of ideas'. His first editorial contrasted ideas, which are 'everything', with facts, which are 'nothing'. He was forgetting that these 'nothings' press upon thinkers with peculiar obstinacy. Each issue carried this slogan beneath its title: 'Vigorous hatred of anarchy; deep and tender love of the people.'

After the supplementary elections of June 1848, at the same time as Hugo entered the Assembly, so did Prince Louis-Napoleon Bonaparte. This son of Hortense Beauharnais and (possibly) a Dutch admiral had not one drop of Bonaparte blood in his veins, but he bore the magic name, and the crowds on the boulevards would chant, 'Po-lé-on, nous l'aurons.' Hugo found him melancholy and ugly, with the look of a sleepwalker; but distinguished, serious, mild, good company and prudent.

L'Événement, following *La Presse*, harnessed itself to the Prince's chariot. Until the October encounter, the Hugo family's newspaper had been cool. Recognizing the prestige of the name, it emphasized that this prestige properly belonged to the uncle and not to the nephew. On 28 October the attitude of *L'Événement* suddenly changed, and in a long article it conferred on the Prince the destiny of France and the Emperor's glory.

In spite of the investiture of the rue de Poitiers, Hugo remained the man of *Les Misérables*. Never trusting to any witness but his own eyes, he had visited the district of Saint-Antoine, and the slums of Lille as well, in order to observe poverty at first hand. He chose not only to talk about it but to denounce the cruel things he heard. There was a fine outcry. What! A member of the party of order who dared say: 'I am one of those who believe that poverty can be wiped out'!

The rupture with the 'burgraves' was complete; the rupture with the Élysée Palace was not long in following. Louis-Napoleon had too lively a taste for duplicity to be able to approve of a policy of dropping bricks. He expressed his desire, at the last moment, for 'a moderate attitude'. Victor Hugo was upsetting his plans by this violence. The one had his ambitions; the other, his convictions. It is said by some that harsh words were exchanged between poet and president.

The two years 1850 and 1851 were for Victor Hugo a period of political battles and emotional tumult. In politics, since the break with the Élysée, he was out on a limb. Though acclaimed by the Left for his brilliant support and

Louis-Napoleon
in 1848

fine speeches in favour of liberty, he was never received as one of them; at the same time he was hooted by the Right, which pretended to despise him as a turncoat and submitted him to an incredible mixture of insult and calumny. He was learning to his cost, as Lamartine had done before him, that of all things popularity is the most fragile.

He would have been in a stronger position in his public life if his private one had been less chaotic and open to criticism. Duty, gratitude, love and desire made him a slave to old liaisons and new adventures alike. Three women, three wives almost, Adèle, Juliette and Léonie, lived in a close circle round him on the slopes of Montmartre, where he had moved in October 1848, to 37 rue de la Tour d'Auvergne. He had to give a portion of his time to each, and went from one to the other; always liable, with Juliette on his arm, to meet Adèle or Léonie – who had up to a point joined forces against the best one of the trio. Juliette, who still followed, under cover, the movements of her lord and master, hid, as Louis Guimbaud put it, 'her humble person and her great love' in the cité Rodier, a gloomy cul-de-sac where she lived 'in an atmosphere of changeless absence and boredom'. Her only pleasure was to visit occasionally the Assembly or the Académie Française with her lover; to hear his speeches; to wait for his rare visits; and to go every morning and look from a distance at the windows of his room. In 1845 he had at last given her permission to go out alone, on foot. She was still ignorant of the part played by Léonie d'Aunet in Victor Hugo's life, and she distrusted other women. In that she was not mistaken; for he was less capable than ever of refusing any woman who offered herself to him.

The former Mme Biard now began to feel that she had ruined her life for Victor Hugo, that she deserved a larger part in his, and that he ought, at least, to give up Juliette. She had often tried to obtain this sacrifice from her lover only to meet with curt refusal. In 1849, for the first time, she threatened Hugo, saying she would reveal everything to Juliette. He snubbed her.

Two years later, Léonie d'Aunet finally struck. On 29 June 1851 a packet of letters arrived at 20 cité Rodier. They were tied up with ribbon and sealed with the arms of Victor Hugo, and bore the motto he himself had invented: *Ego Hugo*. The handwriting was that of the man Juliette adored and venerated. She opened the packet anxiously, read avidly, and learned with horror that since 1844 her lover had loved another woman and had written passionate letters to her, as beautiful as those which for eighteen years had been her only happiness and her only pride. Juliette went out in tears and roamed Paris all day in a state of frenzy. Hugo denied nothing, begged Juliette's forgiveness, and offered to sacrifice her rival to her. But this offer was accompanied by praise of the latter's merits, her beauty and her learning, and hints at the sympathy and affection entertained by the poet's wife and sons for Mme d'Aunet; and this aggravated the bitterness of the situation for Juliette. She was too proud to accept a love which would involve such a renunciation.

They vied with each other in generosity. When Juliette, after sad considera-tion, spoke of parting, Hugo, like all men in a similar position, appealed to her compassion. Then, since both the poet and his mistress were still Romantics; since he had proclaimed the rights of passion; since he was a past master at transmuting his pleasures into mystical effusions; and since he could, when he wished to, be 'gay, easygoing, lovable, enchanting', Juliette, again infatuated, agreed that all three of them should undergo a 'trial period', after which Hugo must choose. For Victor Hugo, the 'trial', which consisted of 'making two women walk across the suspension bridge of love in order to test its strength', was a pleasant enough one. In the mornings he would work at home, while Juliette, at her flat, copied out Jean Valjean, and then joined him under the porch of Notre-Dame de Lorette and accompanied him on his afternoon excursions. Dinner time belonged to the family; the evening to Léonie, of whom he would speak on the following morning to Juliette with wounding enthusiasm and liveliness. But when a trial has four months to go, destiny sees to it that well before the day of decision, that decision is imposed by indirect and unforeseeable means. Thus Hugo was going through a period of more than normal difficulty. Since February 1851 he had taken up a position not only against the government but against Louis-Napoleon personally.

The leaders of the faction surrounding the President were strongly in favour of a *coup de force*. Nor was Louis-Napoleon hostile to it; but he did not wish to risk it before he had provided himself with all possible safeguards. Already the Law, now devoid of justice, was prosecuting the publishers of *L'Événement*. There were sentences of nine months' prison for François-Victor Hugo, the same for Paul Meurice and six months for Auguste Vacquerie. Charles Hugo was already in prison. Then *L'Événement*, which had been banned, reappeared under the name *L'Avènement du Peuple*. Every day Victor Hugo joined his two sons and his two friends imprisoned in the Conciergerie. He drank with them the coarse red wine from the canteen. Soon, no doubt, it would be his turn.

In his private life, too, uncompromising measures were needed; the 'love trial' was beginning to go in Juliette's favour.

3 December 1851 was a day of barricades. Baudin died on one of them with the now famous remark: 'You shall see how a man can die for twenty-five

The Conciergerie, at the time of the imprisonment there of Victor Hugo's sons

francs.' In the place de la Bastille Hugo was delivering a frenzied harangue to a group of officers and police when Juliette, who throughout these days had followed him everywhere, clutched at his arm saying: 'You'll get yourself shot.'

The decisive day was 4 December, the day of the massacre. A bourgeois and liberal opposition had been organized; it was repressed with cruelty. In Paris at least four hundred persons were killed. In the midst of this bloody disorder, Juliette continued to follow Hugo with dog-like devotion. There is something pathetic and sublime in the idea of this woman, still beautiful though worn and grey-haired, shadowing her man at a little distance in order to fling herself if necessary between him and the threat of death. Venturing into the thick of the fighting, she lost him and then found him again. 'Mme Drouet gave everything for me', wrote Victor Hugo, 'it was thanks to her admirable devotion that I survived those days of December 1851.'

Exile   Nevertheless, he had to get out of the country. On Thursday 11 December Victor Hugo left Paris by way of the Gare du Nord, under the name of 'Lanvin (Jacques-Firmin), compositor, living in Paris at 4 rue des Jeûneurs. Age: 48 years. Height: 1 m. 70. Hair: greying. Eyebrows: brown. Eyes: brown. Beard: greying. Chin: round. Face: oval.' The traveller wore a workman's cap and a black coat. Was he unrecognizable? Or was it that they did not want to see through his disguise? Who knows? That they had wished to arrest him during the disturbances was certain. Young Adèle, in a letter to her father, speaks of 'the terrible night when they came for you'. But his flight was less dangerous to the government than the necessity of taking action against him. Juliette, alone in Brussels with the proscribed fugitive, had emerged triumphant from her ordeal by fire.

Compared to the life he had been leading, exile came as a shock, a salutary one. Victor Hugo, peer of France, loaded with honours, the close friend of an old and sceptical king and an easy prey to female admiration, had almost been trapped. Events quite suddenly gave him his chance.

To permit him to play his part to perfection, a lofty poverty best befitted the banished poet. When 'Firmin Lanvin' got off the train at Brussels on 12 December 1851, Laure Luthereau, a friend of Juliette, warned by her of his arrival, took him to shabby hotels – first to the Hôtel du Limbourg, and then to the Hôtel de la Porte-Verte at 31 rue de la Violette. On 14 December Juliette arrived; Victor Hugo met her in the customs shed. She brought his manuscripts. There was an etiquette to be observed in exile; an important refugee could not decently live with his mistress, and Juliette, feeling both hurt and resigned, had to go and live apart from him. She moved in with her friends, the Luthereaus, in the passage du Prince.

From the very beginning there was plenty of copying for Juliette to do. Righteous anger, 'a violent desire to bear witness', possessed Hugo and sought an outlet. He was determined to 'sound the brazen chord'; to become the fierce

The house in the Grande Place, Brussels, where the poet lived in 1852 ▶

conscience of France, 'the man of duty'. First of all he had to write an account of 2 December (it was later entitled *Histoire d'un Crime*). He began it on the morning after his arrival. In Paris Adèle behaved like the dignified wife of an exile. She was prouder of her husband's political role than she had been of his literary fame. Of course, she felt irritated by the presence of Juliette in Brussels. At the same time she continued to countenance and protect the bland Léonie d'Aunet.

In Brussels, Victor Hugo worked with the keenness and enthusiasm which come from passionate feelings. He decided to write and publish as quickly as possible a short pamphlet, *Napoléon le Petit*. This was a simmering improvization, an indictment in the great Latin tradition; it had the rhythm of Cicero, the vigour of Tacitus, the poetry of Juvenal. This discontinuous, rhythmical 'poet's prose' partook of the controlled madness of poetic beauty. Its tone was

Marine Terrace, the first house Victor Hugo lived in at the start of his exile in Jersey

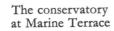

The conservatory
at Marine Terrace

Lancon beach, Jersey,
a lithograph dating
from the time of Victor
Hugo's stay on the island

reminiscent now of the prophets' invective, now of Swift's terrible humour.

It became clear that once *Napoléon le Petit* was published, it would be dangerous for Hugo to allow his family and possessions to remain in France. The government had just published an edict against libel emanating from Frenchmen abroad, threatening them with fines and confiscation. Hence his determination to bring all his dependants to Brussels if the Belgians were still willing to afford him asylum after this outburst, or, failing that, to Jersey. His wife's advice was to sell the lease of the house in the rue de la Tour d'Auvergne, and to auction the 'magnificent Gothic furniture', all the bric-a-brac (which she detested), and the library. The sale by public auction of the family possessions might have proved painful, but for Hugo the pleasure of public sacrifice was like a blessing. The decision was taken. On 25 July Hugo urged his wife to go straight to St Helier, Jersey. He himself, anticipating the Faider Law which would have expelled him, and not wanting to force Belgium to carry the dangerous burden of *Napoléon le Petit*, left with Charles on 1 August.

August 1852. On a burning summer's day three travellers, Mme Victor Hugo, her daughter Adèle, and her attendant knight Auguste Vacquerie, disembarked in Jersey. They had come by way of Southampton, and had loathed their first 'rosbif'. They felt that St Helier with its burnt-out look was terribly like St Helena. Two days later Hugo and Charles joined them at the Pomme d'Or hotel. The exiles, who were fairly numerous but less important than those at Brussels, went to the harbour to meet the poet and, joined by some of the local inhabitants, gave him a resounding welcome.

Hugo wanted to be near the sea. He rented a very isolated house called Marine Terrace, a pretty little villa with a veranda, a flower garden and a kitchen garden. Juliette arrived by another steamer (propriety and Adèle demanded this). She stayed at the inn at first, and then found a small flat.

The microcosm of these two households depended for its existence on a single pen and a single brain. Something must be published, but what? It was best, in these days of anger, to stick to the vein which had inspired *Napoléon le Petit*. The book was being smuggled into France in sections, printed on thin paper, concealed in the linings of garments, and sometimes in hollow busts of Napoleon III, and it was arousing great enthusiasm.

'Les Châtiments' What name should he give to a collection of poems against 'The Crime'? Hugo hesitated. *Le Chant du Vengeur*, *Les Vengeresses*, *Rimes Vengeresses*, *Châtiments* (without the article), and then finally *Les Châtiments*. The book contains a prodigious variety of tone. One strong emotion, that of indignation, gives it its unity. Doubtless it is possible in discussing it to compare it to Aubigné's *Les Tragiques*, to the satire of Menippus, to Tacitus, and above all to Juvenal; but in forcefulness, in newness of rhythm, in beauty of language, in ironic effect, and above all in epic quality, Hugo's collection bears the palm. Such then was the book which grew, page by page of dense, handsome handwriting, during the winter of 1852–3.

Between 1853 and 1856, in growing exaltation, he wrote not only the religious poems, *Les Contemplations*, but a large part of his two immense theological poems, *La Fin de Satan* and *Dieu*. Religions, empires, space, time – the breadth of his vision as he surveyed them has been equalled only by Dante and Milton. In *La Fin de Satan* he portrays the fall of an archangel into darkness, and expresses the passion of Christ in admirable verse. As for the poem called *Dieu*, it is a voyage of the mind among the stars, the centuries, and the creeds.

The situation of the political refugee is a difficult one. He is tolerated rather than adopted. And if the policy of the country of his exile requires some rapprochement with his country of origin, the proscribed man is sacrificed. The authorities in Jersey had never much liked this small group of talkative

Illustration from J. Hetzel's edition of *Les Châtiments*, published in 1872, nineteen years after the first edition

Frenchmen, or this poet who alternated between his wife and his mistress. In the House of Commons Sir Robert Peel had shown unremitting hostility towards Hugo since 1854. In 1855 the situation became acute: the Emperor of the French and the Queen of England, through their alliance against Russia, were becoming friendly.

The Hugos now had to leave Jersey for Guernsey. They departed in several groups. Hugo left first on 31 October, with François-Victor and Juliette Drouet, who was accompanied by her generous-natured maid, Suzanne. Two

Victor Hugo on the Exiles' Rock, Jersey

A view of Guernsey by Georges-Victor Hugo

days after this Charles Hugo joined his father. The two Adèles and Auguste Vacquerie (none of whom were liable to suffer under the expulsion laws, and who had to organize the whole moving operation) arrived later, with thirty-five items of baggage, boxes and bundles. For a moment one heavy trunk hung poised over the stormy waves before being flung into a boat. It contained, in manuscript, *Les Contemplations, Les Misérables, La Fin de Satan, Dieu*, and *Les Chansons des Rues et des Bois*. Never were so many immortal works in more imminent danger of total loss. The island of Guernsey was smaller than Jersey and sloped more abruptly. 'A rock sequestered in the sea.' At that time Victor Hugo's resources were small. No royalties were forthcoming. *Napoléon le Petit* and *Les Châtiments*, books written for the struggle, had been sold surreptitiously and had profited only their distributors. Hugo immediately set to work again.

As soon as a writer has clean paper and a table he has everything. For the others, whom he advised to redouble their economies, it was more difficult.

Then the miracle of *Les Contemplations* intervened. He had in his desk drawers – or rather in his boxes – getting on for eleven thousand lines of poetry, some of them from former days, those of his vanished joys, and some from the present, poems of recollection and meditation. Hetzel, his 'dear fellow-proscript', was anxious to undertake the work of publishing them. Hugo wanted to strike a real blow by publishing the whole lot in two volumes, thus overwhelming his enemies with a broadside of masterpieces.

The success of *Les Contemplations*, unexpected, since no one knew what kind of reception awaited the absent and rebellious poet in the France of the Second Empire, was tremendous. The first edition was sold as soon as it appeared. All lovers of poetry agreed that here were some of the finest lines in the French language. Hugo had carefully organized this scattered collection. With a wise regard for symmetry he had divided it into two sections: 1831–43 and 1843–56. His daughter's death marked the dividing line, and the book passed from a blue and tender past ('*Autrefois*') to a dark and gloomy present ('*Aujourd'hui*').

The book's financial success was equal to its literary one. With the twenty thousand francs in royalties which Hetzel presently sent him, Hugo bought Hauteville House on 10 May. It was paid for wholly by *Les Contemplations*.

He liked the idea of owning property in Guernsey, paid the 'poulade' fee, and by so doing could no longer be expelled from the island.

For Mme Hugo, and even more so for her daughter, this putting down of roots was a cause of sadness. It was as if their exile had been recognized as something permanent. Hugo rose at dawn, awakened by the cannon of the nearby fort, he worked until eleven, in the heat of the sun, then stripped, poured ice-cold water all over himself, and rubbed himself with a friction glove. Passers-by, knowing the great man's peculiar habits, stared at this phenomenon. At noon they lunched. Charles and his father conversed; Mme Hugo admired

◀ Hugo and
August Vacquerie
in Guernsey

Hauteville House,
Guernsey, bought by
Victor Hugo

A dinner given by the Hugos for the poor children of the island.
From left to right: Paul Chenay, the writer's brother-in-law;
Hennet de Kesler; Victor Hugo; Mme Victor Hugo

the genius of 'her men'. Then each one went to his own part of the house.

The *mille passus* were still reserved for Juliette. She had been found a charming little villa called La Fallue, so near to Hauteville House that she could see her demigod at his toilet on the veranda. Each morning she watched the process in order to feast her eyes once more on this body she loved so well. After lunch Hugo would come to fetch her. More often than not she was ordered to walk beside him in silence, and she was apt to complain of this.

The success of *Les Contemplations* discovered many well-wishers in Paris. Praises flowed to Guernsey. Michelet, Dumas, Louise Colet, Père Enfantin, and George Sand all expressed their admiration.

Hetzel, following the publication of *Les Contemplations*, begged Hugo to keep back the philosophical poems *Dieu* and *La Fin de Satan*. On the other hand, Hetzel liked the idea of the *Petites Epopées*, a series of historical frescoes set between the thirteenth and nineteenth centuries. That the nature of Hugo's talent was epic was evident from the irresistible movement, the scale and the sublimity of these poems.

Charles and François-Victor photographed with Victor Hugo in Jersey in 1860

The oak gallery
on the first floor
of Hauteville House

Manuscript page of *Après la Bataille*, one of the poems in *La Légende des Siècles*

The first *Légende des Siècles* was written wholly between 1857 and 1859. It posesses great unity of inspiration. It develops over the whole course of history, but Hugo's imagination was of that vast kind which can encompass the whole 'wall of the centuries' at a glance.

La Légende des Siècles was full of such beauty as must eventually convince even the most hostile readers of the poet's unique greatness. 'Only Victor Hugo has spoken; other men merely stammer', said Jules Renard.

In 1859 the Empire offered an amnesty. Some of the proscripts accepted it. Hugo refused. This great voice crying in the wilderness was to save the reputation of liberty in France, as well as the love of grandiose ideas and great

'La Légende des Siècles'

A page from *La Légende des Siècles* with a drawing by Hugo himself, and a dedication to Paul Meurice

General Hugo, the hero of *Après la Bataille*. Painting by Melingue

Madame Victor Hugo, aged sixty

Victor Hugo in 1861

images, at a time when literature, under the Second Empire, was becoming worldly and frivolous. The French knew this, and for them Victor Hugo now took his place in the 'Legend of the Centuries'.

Absorbed during the decade 1860–70 in immense activity: poems, epics, novels, essays, and *Les Misérables*, which was all these at once, he found in his work a strange happiness, composed of fullness, strength and isolation. *'Les Misérables'*

But he did not notice as he rejoiced in his strength, that those who were close to him were restive. Mme Hugo left Guernsey more and more often. Since she was not happy, she felt the need for distraction, and liked, whether in France or England, to stand proxy for her husband's glory. Her daughter Adèle, who was moody and difficult, sulked, brooded, and lapsed into day-dreaming. At the end of 1864 Charles left Paris to set up house in Brussels. On 17 October 1865, at Saint-Josse-ten-Noode, he married the god-daughter of Jules Simon, Alice Lehaene.

Mme Hugo went with her son to Brussels. This time her absence was to last two years. From January 1865 to January 1867 she did not return to Hauteville House. The old magician was from this time almost alone on his rock. His sister-in-law came to keep house for him. Julie Foucher had married an engraver, Paul Chenay, but they got on badly together. As for Juliette Drouet, she remained loyally at her post. The more his own family abandoned the *paterfamilias*, the more the old lover belonged to his faithful mistress.

Since the age of thirty Hugo had planned and worked on a great social novel. The injustice of punishments, the redemption of the condemned, the portrayal of suffering, the influence of the saintly – these themes were already in his mind in the days of *Le Dernier Jour d'un Condamné*, *Claude Gueux*, and poems such as *Pour les pauvres*. In 1840 he had worked out a preliminary plan for this novel: *Les Misères*, story of a saint — story of a man — story of a woman — story of a doll. That was the way the wind of fashion was blowing in this period. George Sand, Eugène Sue, and even Alexandre Dumas and Frédéric Soulié, were writing novels on the privations of the common people.

During these protracted labours Juliette was a firm and constant support. She loved the book, and copying it gave her very great pleasure. At last it was completed. Victor Hugo wrote to Auguste Vacquerie: 'This morning, 30 June 1861, at half-past eight, with glorious sunlight streaming through my windows, I finished *Les Misérables*.' He knew that it was a great work and that it would be read by an enormous public, and he wanted to take full advantage of this in order to ensure, permanently, the future of those near to him. Which publisher should he choose? Hetzel was his friend and he liked him, but he considered him unbusinesslike. A young Belgian publisher, Albert Lacroix, proposed that he should publish it, and accepted the author's terms; three hundred thousand francs for twelve years' exclusive rights. It was the first time Hugo had ever received such a sum. The book was a triumph. Lacroix made five hundred and seventeen thousand francs net profit between 1862 and 1868. In

Brussels a banquet was organized in honour of *Les Misérables*. The critics were less enthusiastic. Political passions can sometimes influence people's judgment.

But by now, time itself has passed judgment. *Les Misérables* is accepted everywhere as one of the great works of the human mind. Jean Valjean and Cosette have taken their places in that not very large group of heroes of novels that have universal validity.

Théophile Gautier used to say of *Les Misérables* 'it is neither good nor bad; it is not a human product but something created by the elements.' This remark really applies more to some of the other works of the period of exile, notably to *William Shakespeare*, 'an epic, oceanic work of criticism', a stream of lava from which emerge giant statues, still glowing with sombre fires. Hugo had three reasons for concerning himself with Shakespeare; 1864 would be the tercentenary year, and because of that the subject was again a topical one; François-Victor had asked him for a preface to his own translation; and above all, he felt the need, forty years after *Cromwell*, to replace the manifesto with a balance-sheet which would be the literary testament at once of the nineteenth century and of the Romantic movement.

The real subject of the book is that of genius, or rather, of geniuses. Those he places on the level of Shakespeare are Homer, Job, Aeschylus, Isaiah, Ezekiel, Lucretius, Juvenal, Tacitus, St John, Dante, Rabelais, Cervantes. Only one Frenchman.

Javert. An illustration by Brion for Hetzel's edition of *Les Misérables* (1865)

Jean Valjean. An illustration for the same edition

Gavroche aged eleven. A drawing by Victor Hugo

William Shakespeare was published in 1864; in 1865 *Les Chansons des Rues et des Bois* surprised the detractors of the apocalyptic poet and Promethean critic by suddenly recalling the sensuous and jovial Hugo. He had been in love with love all his life, and taken pleasure in singing of it.

It was, then, an enchanting and well ordered ballet in which danced the most beautiful words in the language; a Watteau-Chénier-Theocritus production, where idylls are inscribed on pier-glasses, and nymphs follow washerwomen onto the stage. A clash of cymbals, and the genial ballet-master turns to demonstrate to the reader that even at this speed he can change without difficulty from idyll to epic. The worldly public of the Second Empire turned the book into a best-seller. Its feeling, gracefully licentious, was that of the age. But ordinary people who had read and appreciated *Les Châtiments* were not interested in this erudite poetry.

The year 1867 saw an event which in Juliette's eyes was a great one: a visit on the part of Mme Hugo to Hauteville Féerie, that is to say to Mme Drouet. From this moment on, Juliette acquired 'the delightful habit of sharing in the

Frontispiece to *Les Travailleurs de la Mer*, published in 1866

family affections'. A little later she spent three months in Brussels with her beloved, and was received at the house in the place des Barricades. She was even invited, with Charles, his wife, and their four-month-old son, little Georges, to spend a few weeks in the country, in the woods of Chaudfontaine. While there, she read to Mme Hugo, who was suffering from eyestrain.

A new rhythm of life was established. Mme Hugo lived mainly in Paris, where from time to time Charles's family would ask for her hospitality. In Brussels, François-Victor, together with Charles and Alice, ran the house in the place des Barricades; Mme Hugo's sister, Julie Chenay, together with Juliette, watched over the great exile in Guernsey. In summer the Hugo family foregathered in Brussels.

All this while Hugo was working and creating. In 1866 he published a long novel, *Les Travailleurs de la Mer*. He admired huge edifices and took pleasure in thinking of this book as a stone in the giant edifice of *anankè* (destiny, fate). It was on the island of Sark, where he had gone in 1859 with Juliette and Charles, that he had first observed the methods used by sailors to scale cliffs;

'Les Travailleurs de la Mer'

End of the breakwater, Guernsey. Pen-and-ink drawing by Victor Hugo

the rocky caves of the smugglers, and the octopus, which was to supply him with such a dramatic combat. Storms, sketched in his notebooks, would also serve for the book, which was at first entitled *Gilliatt le Marin*.

François-Victor Hugo to his father: 'Your success is enormous, universal. I have never seen such unanimity. Even the triumph of *Les Misérables* has been exceeded. This time the master has found a public worthy of him. You have been understood, and that means everything. Because to understand a work like that is to admire it. Your name is in all the newspapers, on every wall, in every shop window, on everyone's lips. . . .'

Le Soleil, which was re-publishing the novel in serial form, increased its own circulation (despite the previous publication of the book) from 28,000 to 80,000 copies. The press dared admit to being enthusiastic. This book at least did not arouse political antagonism.

Since the *coup d'état*, no play by Victor Hugo, an enemy of the régime, had been performed in Paris. Then came 1867, the year of the Exposition Universelle. It was a question of showing the world the finest that France had to offer. Lacroix published a *Paris-Guide* with a preface by Hugo. Could the Comédie-Française reject one of its great authors at a time like this? A new production of *Hernani* was proposed. Victor Hugo felt some misgivings.

Its success was 'untellable' (the adjective is Adèle's), nevertheless tell it she did: 'Everyone was in a frenzy. People embracing each other – even in the square in front of the theatre. The youth of today was even more enthusiastic than that of 1830. It showed itself to be superb, valiant, ready for anything. I am happy, I am in heaven. . . .' In the audience were Dumas, Gautier, Banville, Girardin, Jules Simon, Paul Meurice, Adolphe Crémieux, Auguste Vacquerie. The gallery was packed with youngsters from the lycées.

Charles would have liked to stay in Paris and found a newspaper, but was it an opportune moment? The *paterfamilias*, when consulted about it, said that he would not risk a halfpenny in such an enterprise. Hugo was working on a new novel, *Par ordre du Roi*. Charles tried to persuade his brother to join him in Paris. Life was so pleasant there.

But François-Victor meant to remain loyal to exile. The summer of 1868 approached, and with it the time for the family gathering in Brussels. Mme Hugo treated seeing her husband again as a celebration: 'As for me, once I have you I shall fasten on to you without asking your permission. I shall be so sweet and so kind that you will not want to leave me. My final wish is to die in your arms.' As she grew weaker, she clung to the strength which had so often terrified her.

Death of Mme Hugo Her wish was granted. On 29 August 1868 she went for a drive with her husband in an open carriage, he very tender, she very gay. The next day, towards three o'clock in the morning, she had an attack of apoplexy. Her breath came in a whistle, she suffered from convulsions and partial paralysis. *Victor Hugo's Diary*, 27 August 1868: 'Died this morning, at half past six. I

General view of the Exposition Universelle, held in Paris in 1867

closed her eyes. Alas! God will take this sweet and noble soul to himself. I give her up to him. Bless her! We shall carry out her wish to be taken to Villequier and buried close to our dear dead daughter. I shall go with the coffin as far as the frontier. . . .'

He returned immediately to his laborious and ordered life at Hauteville House. Every Monday there was the dinner for the forty poor children. Every evening, 'dinner at Hauteville II. It will be so every day now, *Deo volente*. . . .'

And from dawn to dusk, work. He continued 'to pile Pelion on Ossa'. Hugo was a sexagenarian, and yet he announced a series of future novels: *L'Homme qui rit* (or England after 1688); France before 1789 (title undecided); *Quatrevingt-Treize*. Aristocracy; monarchy; democracy. For *L'Homme qui rit* he had long sought the proper title. He had told Lacroix, who was to publish it, that it would be *Par ordre du Roi*. Then, on his friend's advice, *L'Homme qui rit*. Was it a historical novel? It was simultaneously, he said, 'drama and history. There will be an unexpected view of England. The period is that extraordinary time between 1688 and 1705. It prepares us for our own eighteenth century in France.'

L'Homme qui rit was less successful than the previous novels, partly through Lacroix's fault – he turned the occasion into a bookselling enterprise of rather too commercial a kind – but also because the Realist and Naturalist writers had given the public a taste for the drama of everyday life.

In 1869 certain rumblings announced the end of the régime in France. Military disaster in Mexico and diplomatic defeat in Europe had annoyed and humiliated Frenchmen. The Emperor, tired and sick, was surrendering ground. The former editors of *L'Événement* (Hugo's two sons, Paul Meurice, and Auguste Vacquerie) decided that the moment had come to found a newspaper to attack the Second Empire. They recruited two brilliant polemicists, Henri Rochefort and Édouard Lockroy, the son of the actor. They looked for a title. Victor Hugo suggested *L'Appel au Peuple*. They preferred *Le Rappel*. It came out on 8 May 1869 and its circulation at once reached fifty thousand.

Lively and irreverent, the paper was a success. Victor Hugo encouraged the combatants from Guernsey. In September he accepted an invitation to go to Lausanne for the Peace Conference. On his return he thought he would like to visit Switzerland with Juliette. He was happy to see again the head-waters of the Rhine at Schaffhausen.

He still worked according to his inflexible timetable, but this activity was like the panic of the last days before a departure, when one finishes in haste the work in progress, and feels already separated from the place one is in. Everyone felt confusedly that something was about to happen. 'Liberty crowned the edifice at the very moment its foundations crumbled.' In May 1870 there was a plebiscite on the reforms. Seven-and-a-half million 'yes' votes seemed to have consolidated the 'liberal Empire'.

Franco-Prussian War   In Europe, Bismarck was seeking war. For Hugo, war raised a question of conscience. A victorious Empire would mean the consolidation of the man of 2 December. A vanquished Empire would mean the humiliation of France. Ought he to go back as a member of the National Guard and die as a Frenchman, forgetting the fact of the Empire? With Juliette's assistance, he packed his bags. He would go to Brussels in any case. On 9 August it became clear that the war was fast becoming a catastrophe. Three battles were lost one after the other.

Poster issued by the Commune of 23 May 1871 ▶

RÉPUBLIQUE FRANÇAISE

LIBERTÉ — EGALITÉ — FRATERNITÉ

COMMUNE DE PARIS

LE PEUPLE DE PARIS
AUX SOLDATS DE VERSAILLES

FRÈRES!

L'heure du grand combat des Peuples contre leurs oppresseurs est arrivée!

N'abandonnez pas la cause des Travailleurs!

Faites comme vos frères du 18 mars!

Unissez-vous au Peuple, dont vous faites partie!

Laissez les aristocrates, les privilégiés, les bourreaux de l'humanité se défendre eux-mêmes, et le règne de la Justice sera facile à établir.

Quittez vos rangs!

Entrez dans nos demeures.

Venez à nous, au milieu de nos familles. Vous serez accueillis fraternellement et avec joie.

Le Peuple de Paris a confiance en votre patriotisme.

VIVE LA RÉPUBLIQUE!
VIVE LA COMMUNE!

3 prairial an 79.

LA COMMUNE DE PARIS.

IMPRIMERIE NATIONALE. — Mai 1871.

On 15 August he embarked with Juliette, Charles, Alice, the children, Jeanne's nursemaid and three servants. By 18 August they were all at the place des Barricades.

On 19 October he went to the Chancellery of the French Embassy to ask for a passport for Paris.

Return to Paris

On 3 September the Emperor capitulated, and on the 4th a Republic was proclaimed. On the 5th Victor Hugo, at the booking office of the railway station in Brussels, asked in a voice trembling with emotion for 'a ticket to Paris'. He had on a soft felt hat, and was carrying a leather satchel slung from his shoulder. He looked at the clock to see the hour that marked the end of his exile, and, looking very pale, said to Jules Claretie, a young writer who was with him: 'I have been waiting for this moment for nineteen years.' The train

Guns in Montmartre during the siege of Paris, 1870–1

A corner of the Marché St Germain showing a poulterer's stall selling cat and dog meat during the siege

arrived at 9.35. There was an enormous crowd waiting. His welcome was indescribable.

Théophile Gautier's daughter Judith was there. On the arm of this beautiful girl he managed to get to a small café opposite the station. From a first-floor balcony, and later from his carriage, the great proscript had to speak four times. There were shouts of 'Vive Victor Hugo!' and people recited lines from *Les Châtiments*. The crowd wanted to take him to the Hôtel de Ville. A tremendous thunderstorm broke that night. Heaven itself took part.

At his destination, Paul Meurice's house in the avenue Frochot, Hugo had innumerable callers. On his arrival he had written an 'Appeal to the Germans'. When he saw the ring of steel tightening round Paris, he became fierce. In many of the theatres there were readings from *Les Châtiments*, the profits from which were to go towards buying guns for the Army of Paris. Their success was such that the committee was able to buy three guns, which were named Châteaudun, Châtiments and Victor Hugo. Actors came to rehearse at the avenue Frochot. Victor Hugo saw Frédérick Lemaître, Lia Félix and Marie Laurent. He was happy to find himself once again in this theatrical atmosphere, so alive and intoxicating that no one who has once breathed it can ever forget it.

In the streets soldiers of the line, militiamen and snipers, often carrying vegetables collected under enemy fire, could be seen passing. The shops became bare. Workmen in caps and smocks shouted 'Vive La Commune!' A retreat was sounded. On 31 October the Commune (Blanqui, Flourens) attempted to overthrow the provisional government. Like all Parisians, Hugo did not have much to eat. 'They make pies from rats. They are said to be good.' The zoo at the Jardin des Plantes sent him bear's flesh and deer and antelope meat.

The bombardment was gutting Paris. The district of his childhood, the Feuillantines, suffered. A shell smashed the Chapel of the Virgin at Saint-Sulpice, where Hugo had been married. Supporters of the Commune pressed the poet more and more strongly to help them overthrow the government, which he now despised. However, he thought an uprising in the face of the enemy would be even more dangerous for the country than the continuation of this impotent authority, 'this dwarf who boasted that he could father a child on this giantess, France'. In the beginning, Paris had accepted the siege with joyful courage, but the heroic comedy had turned tragic. Famine gripped the city. Shells whistled. In the distance Saint-Cloud burned red. Counter-attacks at Champigny and Montretout failed, 'owing to the incapacity of the leaders' said the Parisians. On the evening of 28 January there was an armistice. It was snowing, as in *L'Expiation*. The relentless Bismarck declared: 'The animal is dead.' Paris saw the return of poultry meat; but it also witnessed the arrival of the spiked helmets.

A National Assembly had to be elected to make peace. It would sit at Bordeaux. Naturally Victor Hugo stood as a candidate in the department of the Seine. He left for Bordeaux, certain that he would be elected. Although the idea of belonging to the Assembly which was to ratify defeat did not please him, he could not avoid it.

In this city invaded by deputies it was difficult to find lodgings, especially for Hugo who never moved without his ménage. Charles and his family found a little flat at 13 rue Saint-Maur; Alice observed that the figure 13 pursued them. They had left on 13 February, there had been thirteen passengers in the saloon car. The poet, who was very superstititous, sensed misfortune.

Gambetta, Louis Blanc, Brisson, Lockroy and Clemenceau rallied round Victor Hugo and made him into a sort of president of the Left.

On 8 March the Assembly discussed the case of Garibaldi. It was proposed that the great Italian's election (in Algeria) be annulled, even though he had placed himself at the service of France in her darkest hour. Hugo protested, amid tumult, and to the rage of the majority: 'Three weeks ago you refused to

The National Assembly of Bordeaux discussing the peace terms of March 1871 ▶

hear Garibaldi. . . . Today you refuse to hear me. That is enough. I am tendering my resignation. . . .'

Death of Charles   For several days Hugo had been sleeping badly. He reflected that he was again about to leave a temporary dwelling-place on 13 March. An evil omen. All day he wandered about Bordeaux, and visited the Palais Gallien. He was due to dine at the Restaurant Lanta with Alice, Charles and three friends. At the appointed time Alice and the other guests were there waiting for Charles. He had taken a cab . . . opening the door at the Café de Bordeaux, the driver had found him dead. Blood poured from his nose and mouth. It was an attack of apoplexy. Hugo decided that his son should be buried in the Père Lachaise cemetery, in General Hugo's family vault. He left Bordeaux on 17 March at six-thirty in the evening with a heavy heart, but courageously.

Charles Hugo's funeral took place in Paris on 18 March 1871 during the revolt against the Assembly

Burning of the Hôtel de Ville (24 May 1871) during the Commune

The funeral train steamed into a Paris in open riot. The Commune was The Commune seizing power. Patriots and revolutionaries were united by their anger against the Assembly and the peace treaty. Rumours flew; there was fighting in Montmartre; two generals had been shot. At the cemetery, Vacquerie pronounced an oration. Before the coffin was lowered, Hugo knelt and kissed it. It was his part of the rites. As he left, the crowd surrounded him. Strangers took him by the hand. 'How this people love me and how I love them!'

Immediately, accompanied by Juliette, Alice and her children, he left for Brussels, where Charles had lived since his marriage, and where he had left a heavily encumbered estate.

Hugo followed events in Paris closely. They were lamentable. Frenchmen were fighting each other under the eyes of the enemy. If Hugo had thought he could serve any useful purpose, he would, he declared, have gone back to Paris in spite of his duty towards his family.

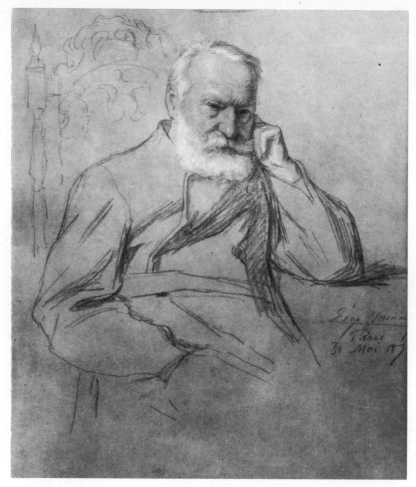

Victor Hugo in 1872, by Flameng

But in Paris, as in Versailles, the spirit of hatred carried all before it. Every day Hugo heard of the death or the arrest of some friend. The victims of the Commune drifted towards Belgium, and Hugo announced that he would shelter the new proscripts at his house (4 place des Barricades). 'Let us not close our doors against the fugitives, who are perhaps innocent, and without doubt unwitting offenders. . . .'

His protest in favour of the right of asylum appeared in *L'Indépendance belge*. He received many letters of congratulation, but was awakened in the night by shouts of 'À mort Victor Hugo! À mort le brigand! À la lanterne!' Stones

Pen and ink drawing by Victor Hugo of the house by the bridge over the
Our at Vianden in Luxembourg, where he lived after the Commune

shattered his windows and his chandeliers. Not a very serious matter really, but
a decree of the Belgian government enjoined 'Victor Hugo, man of letters, aged
sixty-nine, to leave the kingdom at once. He is refused permission to return in
the future.'

It should be said in justice to Belgium that protests against this expulsion
were vehement, both in the Chamber of Representatives and throughout the
country. To return to France at that time would be to expose himself to useless
scenes of violence. He decided to go to Luxembourg. At Vianden he rented two
houses. One of them, ancient and decorated with carving, overlooking the river
Our, was for himself; the other, opposite it, was for his family. He set to work
at once, glad to get back to his novel and his poems, but upset by the news
from Paris. Meurice had been arrested. Vacquerie's safety was threatened;
Rochefort seemed to be destined for deportation. Louise Michel, 'a small, wild,
dreamy creature' shouted at the Council of War: 'If you are not cowards, kill
me!' Hugo wrote some fine verses in her honour, and protested against the
savagery of the reprisals. It was an incredibly productive two months.

On 1 October, he reached Paris: a somewhat sinister homecoming. He went for a drive with Juliette and saw the ruins of the Tuileries and the Hôtel de Ville. He was begged to intervene to save Rochefort. In the first issue of *Le Rappel*, which was at last permitted to reappear, he published a *Letter to the Editors*. The number was at a premium. Hugo's readers remained faithful to him, but the authorities hated him.

The year 1872 seemed to him full of gloom. He was beaten in the January elections. His tolerance towards the Communards had alarmed the voters. Only work and sensuality still had the power to save him from his phantoms. Women continued to play an important part in his life. He was now seventy. A new production of *Ruy Blas* at the Odéon brought him once more into contact with actresses. Juliette was present at the auditions. 'J.-J. was there', wrote Hugo on the 2 January. 'O memory!' The part which Mme Hugo had once caused to be taken away from Juliette, that of the Queen, fell to Sarah Bernhardt, a young, svelte girl with enormous eyes and a voice of gold. From the moment that she met 'the monster' she was infatuated with him.

19 February 1872. Sarah Bernhardt as the Queen in the Odéon production of *Ruy Blas*

Judith Gautier,
after her marriage
to Catulle Mendès

By the opening night, author and actress felt equally affectionate towards each other. But among the countless admirers – society women, actresses, women of letters – who now came to offer themselves and filled his diaries with their photographs (carefully stuck on the backs of certain pages, and often accompanied by pressed flowers), the queen of the hour was Judith Gautier, as Edmond de Goncourt described her: 'beautiful, black-haired, with a skin of a dazzling whiteness only just tinged with pink, and great eyes whose lashes, thick like those of an animal, gave the languorous creature the indefinable, mysterious quality of a sphinx. . . .' He had known and courted her since Brussels, where she had come on a vist with her husband Catulle Mendès. In 1872 she saw Hugo often. It was an intoxicating conquest. He wanted to take Judith to Hauteville House, he wanted to take refuge there. The success of *Ruy Blas* had made all the theatre managers want to put on Hugo plays. 'But rehearsing for one play', he said, 'prevents me from writing another; and since I have only four or five years more in which to create, I wish to carry out the things I still have in my mind. . . . All in all, I had better go away.' *L'Année terrible*, an admirable collection, had been received without great excitement. Hugo was happy when he left for Guernsey on 7 August 1872, stopping briefly in Jersey on the way.

Hauteville House again. It was a joy to come back to the 'look-out', the transparent cell in which he worked, drenched in sunlight and surrounded by dancing waves. Within a few months, he had composed sketches for the *Théâtre en liberté*, sections of the new *Légende des Siècles*, and one of his finest novels, *Quatrevingt-Treize*.

At first the house was made cheerful by the presence of Alice and the children. But a young widow could hardly enjoy this island solitude under the tutelage of her father-in-law's ageing mistress. Mme Charles Hugo was sweet and good-natured. Was it her fault if she was bored?

On 1 October François-Victor (ill with tuberculosis), Alice, Georges and Jeanne sailed for France. *Diary*: 'They get into the carriage. . . . I kiss Jeanne who is surprised and says: "Papapa! Get in!" I close the door. The carriage starts. I watch it as far as the turning. It disappears completely. A terrible wrench.'

Paul Meurice and Édouard Lockroy were pressing him to come back to Paris to exert his political influence. But he knew that Guernsey was best for him: 'I do more here in a week than I could in a month in Paris.' And the quality was equal to the quantity.

He had never been happier working on a novel than he was with *Quatrevingt-Treize*. To write straight ahead had been his method at the time of *Notre-Dame de Paris*, when he was thirty; the septuagenarian had no less vigour or sustained inspiration. *Quatrevingt-Treize* was the conflict of his youth, between the 'Whites' and the 'Blues', taking place not in a human soul, as in the case of Marius in *Les Misérables*, but in action. The background, that of the Royalist insurrection in Brittany, was familiar to him. Juliette copied the book with enthusiasm: 'I am speechless with admiration before the catalogue of your masterpieces.'

On 1 January 1873, she repeated the prayer which he had once composed for her: 'O God, let us live together always – grant this to me; grant it to him. Let him never be absent from a single day of my life or from one instant of my eternity. . . .' But pleasure has powers of attraction greater than the restraining force of vows. *Quatrevingt-Treize* was finished, but now the news from François-Victor became alarming. On 31 July 1873 Hugo took Juliette back to France. Mac-Mahon had just succeeded Thiers; the military were triumphant, and people began to ask: would there be another *coup d'état*? At all events, repression was intensified. He went to live at Auteuil, in the avenue des Sycomores, in the house of his dying son, whom Mme Charles Hugo was nursing with great

'Quatrevingt-Treize'

Frontispiece to *Quatrevingt-Treize* ▶

114

QUATREVINGT TREIZE

PAR

VICTOR HUGO

LES PLACARDS POPULAIRES

VICTOR HUGO et ses deux fils

10^{C.} **10^{C.}**

Victor Hugo

Charles HUGO

François-Victor HUGO

VICTOR HUGO est né à Besançon le 26 février 1802. Son père était le général comte Joseph-Léopold Hugo, c'est-à-dire sortait de la Révolution et de l'Empire. Sa mère, au contraire, appartenait à une famille vendéenne.

De cette double origine vinrent tour à tour et naturellement les deux opinions qu'il eut avant de s'en faire une à lui.

Il fut d'abord royaliste avec sa mère et chanta les Bourbons.

— Laissez faire le temps, disait le général Hugo. L'enfant est de l'opinion de la mère; l'homme sera de l'opinion du père.

Le changement ne se fit pas attendre. Sensible dans l'Ode à son père, se changeant continua par le Chant de l'arc de triomphe de l'Étoile, et éclata comme une trompette guerrière dans l'Ode à la colonne.

Victor Hugo, qui s'était marié quelques années auparavant avec Mlle Adèle Foucher, une compagne d'enfance, ne devait pas, d'ailleurs, s'attarder longtemps avec la légende de l'Empire. Dès 1830, il était républicain et pour toujours, tout en acceptant la royauté mixte de Louis-Philippe, qui lui semblait une transition utile.

Cependant Victor Hugo voulut bientôt prendre une part immédiate à la politique. Il ne pouvait arriver à la Chambre des députés : il se rejeta sur la Chambre des pairs et, pour y atteindre, se présenta à l'Académie. Trois fois ce fut en vain. Enfin il enfonça la porte (1841), et le gouvernement de Juillet saisit la première occasion pour profiter du droit qu'il avait de prendre des pairs dans l'Académie et lui ouvrit les portes du Luxembourg (1845).

Dès lors commença la véritable vie politique de Victor Hugo, incarnation de la lumière et de la liberté, racontée en détail dans notre Victor Hugo homme politique.

Arriva la Révolution de 1848. Victor Hugo défendit jusqu'au dernier moment le gouvernement auquel il avait prêté serment, et, vaincu, reprit son serment intact des mains du peuple.

Les électeurs républicains de Paris ne purent l'envoyer à l'Assemblée nationale; mais ils prirent leur revanche et le firent entrer un des premiers à l'Assemblée constituante.

À l'Assemblée constituante, Victor Hugo parut un des premiers à l'Assemblée législative, et ce fut pour lutter contre Bonaparte, qui ne tarda pas à se faire soupçonner. Il faut lire, entre autres de ses discours, celui du 17 juillet 1851, où il jeta au misérable le nom de « Napoléon le Petit » comme une marque indélébile.

Glorieuse lutte; mais, hélas! Victor Hugo ne put empêcher l'attentat du 2 Décembre de réussir.

Exilé, Victor Hugo reprit la lutte contre Bonaparte et l'Empire, et, quand l'un et l'autre furent tombés dans la boue sanglante de Sedan, il revint à Paris pour prendre sa part des tortures de l'héroïque ville assiégée.

Nommé à l'Assemblée nationale, réunie pour traiter de la paix ou de la guerre, il repoussa toute paix honteuse et donna presque aussitôt sa démission devant l'insulte faite par la droite à Garibaldi.

Élu sénateur le 30 janvier par le département de la Seine, il prit, avec Raspail à la Chambre des députés, l'initiative de la demande d'amnistie, qui fut repoussée.

Benjamin PIFTEAU

CHARLES-VICTOR HUGO

CHARLES-VICTOR HUGO, fils aîné de Victor Hugo, est né à Paris le 2 novembre 1826.

Il fit de brillantes études au lycée Charlemagne, à deux pas de la maison paternelle de la place Royale, 9. Vint la Révolution de 1848, et Lamartine, qui était devenu ministre des affaires étrangères, se l'attacha comme secrétaire. En même temps, il fut l'un des rédacteurs du journal de son père, l'Événement.

C'est que qu'il fit, à propos d'une exécution qui avait eu lieu avec des détails atroces, cet article si éloquemment indigné qu'il le mena en cour d'assises et le fit condamner à six mois de prison, malgré l'admirable plaidoyer de son père lui-même.

Après le coup d'État du 2 Décembre, il suivit son père en exil, faisant parfois seulement quelques excursions artistiques en Normandie.

Cependant, pas plus que son père ni son frère, il ne laissa dormir sa plume.

En 1857, il donna le Cochon de saint Antoine, fantaisie philosophique, en 3 volumes; en 1859, la Bohème dorée, roman de mœurs, en 2 volumes, et la Chaise de paille, autre roman, en 1 vol.; en 1860, Une Famille tragique, roman-feuilleton publié par la Presse.

Depuis, le Rappel publia avec le plus grand succès les Hommes de l'exil, éloquente étude sur ces vaillants citoyens qui, comme Schœlcher et Noël Parfait, avaient fui comme de scène du 2 Décembre; mais le digne fils du grand homme n'était plus.

Il était mort à Bordeaux, où il accompagnait son père, député à l'Assemblée nationale.

Son enterrement, qui eut lieu à Paris le 18 mars 1871, fut l'occasion d'une respectueuse ovation à la douleur paternelle, comme on peut le voir dans notre Victor Hugo homme politique. Il avait épousé la fille d'un éditeur de Bruxelles.

Benjamin PIFTEAU

FRANÇOIS-VICTOR HUGO

FRANÇOIS-VICTOR HUGO, second fils de Victor Hugo, est né à Paris le 22 octobre 1828.

Il fit, comme son frère, ses études au lycée Charlemagne, et elles furent des plus brillantes. On reconnaissait dans ses deux fils l'élève écrivant à 14 ans, pour le concours de l'Académie, les Aramis de l'étude, et recevant un prix des Jeux floraux de Toulouse à 17 ans.

Retiré entre son père et son frère à Jersey, puis à Guernesey, François-Victor fit comme eux : il remplit les longues heures de l'exil par le travail.

Il publia d'abord l'Île de Jersey, ses monuments, son histoire, ou la Normandie inconnue (1857, in-8°), étude d'un véritable mérite; puis, dans la même année, les Sonnets de Shakespeare, traduits pour la première fois en français, avec une introduction remarquable.

Enfin, en 1860, il commença la publication de son œuvre capitale, qu'il avait étudiée et préparée entre les deux Shakespeare, en s'inspirant du premier pour mieux comprendre le second : sa magnifique traduction des Œuvres complètes de Shakespeare, avec une étude sur chaque pièce.

Rentré en France avec son père, il resta pour consoler celui-ci de la perte de son premier fils, quand, bientôt atteint d'une maladie qui ne pardonne pas, il alla rejoindre son aîné, ne laissant plus, pour le retenir à la vie, comme orphelins, que les deux enfants de Charles : Georges et la petite Jeanne.

De même que pour celui qui l'avait précédé dans la tombe, les funérailles de François-Victor (28 déc. 1873) furent l'occasion d'une ovation pour Victor Hugo, qui revint du cimetière en répétant avec douleur les beaux vers des Feuilles d'automne, où il demande à Dieu de ne jamais voir « la cage sans oiseau, la maison sans enfants! »

Benjamin PIFTEAU

Publications de la LIBRAIRIE DE LA RENAISSANCE, 3, rue de la Vieille-Estrapade, 3

Histoire des Montagnards, par A. Esquiros, nouvelle édition complètement remaniée par l'auteur. 70 livraisons à 10 c. ou 14 séries à 50 c. 1 volume broché. 7 fr.

Victor Hugo homme politique, par B. Pifteau. 25 livraisons à 10 c. ou 5 séries à 50 c. 1 volume broché. . . . 2 fr. 50

La souscription est permanente pour ces deux ouvrages.

Les Conspirations sous le second empire (affaire de l'Hippodrome et de l'Opéra-Comique), par Albert Fermé. 1 volume. . . . . . . 1 fr. 50

Histoire de la démocratie angevine, par Armand Rivière. 1 volume. . 1 fr. 50

Démocratisation de la noblesse, par le docteur Lelorr. 1 volume. . 1 fr. 50

Les Plaies sociales, par le docteur Lux (du Réveil). 1 volume. . . . . 4 fr.

kindness. Goncourt saw them there, François-Victor in an armchair, 'his skin waxen, his arms hugging his body, as if he were shivering', and his father standing 'stiffly erect like an old Huguenot in a play'. Françoois-Victr died on 26 December 1873. *Victor Hugo's Diary*: 'Another break, and a severe one, in my life. All I have left now are Georges and Jeanne. . . .' The funeral, like Charles', was a civil ceremony.

Death of François-Victor

On 1 January 1874 Hugo got up at about two o'clock in the morning to write a line which had come to him: 'What am I good for now? Death.' But he knew it was not true. In spite of the axe-blows of fate, the old oak still stood; in spite of all his bereavements, Hugo worked on happily. He never tired of 'accomplishing and strengthening himself in his art. . . . What prodigious lines he wrote in those last years of his life!' says Paul Valéry. 'No other verses can bear any extensive comparison with them in terms of interior organization, resonance, or fullness!'

On 29 April 1874 the family moved to 21 rue de Clichy. Hugo had taken two floors there: one for himself, Alice and the children; on the other were the reception rooms and Mme Drouet's apartments. These rooms were on the third and fourth floors, and Hugo climbed the stairs without getting in the least out of breath. He still had the eyesight of a young man, and was very surprised when, for the first time in his life, he suffered from toothache.

Poor Juliette still tried to defend her long-established love, but the infernal merry-go-round of young mistresses continued.

Erotic ecstacies were not however allowed to break into his working mornings. From dawn neighbours could observe him in his 'inner sanctum', sitting upright at his desk, wearing a red jersey and a grey coat. In the evenings, surrounded by friends, he was, said Flaubert, 'divine'. Edmond de Goncourt, arriving at the rue de Clichy on 27 December 1875, saw him in a velvet-collared frock-coat with a loose white scarf round his neck, stretched out on a divan and talking about the conciliatory part he intended to play henceforth.

Besides literary friends, the rue de Clichy was visited by political ones: Louis Blanc, Jules Simon, Gambetta, Clemenceau. Little by little time calmed men's minds, and people became inclined to forgive the Commune, and Hugo, the man of mercy, now seemed a precursor. Juliette, greedy for his popularity, wished to see him re-enter political life. In January 1876, on Clemenceau's suggestion, he became a candidate for the Senate, and was elected at the second vote.

1877 was a year of political battles. The President of the Council, Jules Simon, a Jew with the temperament of a Roman Cardinal, and a familiar figure at the rue de Clichy, tried in vain to come to an understanding with Mac-Mahon, who found the anticlericalism of Gambetta insufferable. *Victor Hugo's Diary*, 19 September 1877: 'Mac-Mahon's manifesto. This man is challenging France. . . .' A few days before, he had received at the rue de Clichy, at nine o'clock in the morning, the Emperor of Brazil, Don Pedro, who had treated

◀ First issue of *Les Placards populaires*

him as he would once have wished to be treated by the King of France: as an equal. The Senate was buzzing like a bee-hive. On 21 June Hugo made a lengthy and very fine speech against dissolution. He was acclaimed by the Left. The next morning Jeanne (aged eight) came into his room and asked: 'Did it go well at the Senate?' It had, indeed, gone very well, but the speech had as usual convinced only those who had been convinced already.

The dissolution was decided on by 149 votes to 130. In the elections the Republicans won a crushing majority: 326 seats to 200. The Marshal's position was becoming untenable. 'You will have to submit, or else resign', Gambetta told him. Mac-Mahon did first the one and then the other. Victor Hugo's part in the victory of the Left had been limited by his age and by his remoteness from affairs, but it was incontestable nevertheless. Henceforth he took on, says Pierre Audiat, 'the role, in the Third Republic, of patriarch and guide'.

'L'Art d'être Grand-Père'

In 1877 he published *L'Art d'être Grand-Père*. He had always loved children. He understood them, he delighted in their primitiveness, their naturalness, their poetic quality. Tragically bereaved of his own sons and daughters, he had become devoted to his grandchildren. Georges was handsome and serious, Jeanne wayward and gay. Their grandfather played games with them, drew portraits of them, and kept their little shoes, as Jean Valjean had kept those of Cosette as a child. He wrote down the things they said. *L'Art d'être Grand-Père* was partly made up of the notes of the 'adoring and enraptured' grandfather. Its success was immediate. People like emotions to be simple and warm. The first edition sold out in a few days, others quickly followed. Georges and Jeanne became a legend, and Paris admired them rather as London admires its Royal children.

The grandfather's archangelic verses ought not to give us a false impression of Victor Hugo's last days. Adoration of infant purity had not put an end to the old man's escapades. On 11 January 1877 Alice announced to him that after six years of widowhood she was going to marry Édouard Lockroy, Deputy for the Bouches-du-Rhône department, and former secretary to Renan, the pungent and witty journalist.

This marriage gave Victor Hugo greater freedom in his movements. In spite of his seventy-five years he indulged somewhat too freely in it. Not that he was not becoming more and more aware of the unseemliness of an old man in love. He had written an unfinished comedy, *Philémon Perverti*, in which he had dealt severely with his own character. In it Philémon is not restrained by the sorrow of the tender Baucis but surrenders to the charms of the young Eglé.

He overdid things in other directions: by preparing for publication *L'Histoire d'un Crime*, which he regarded as more topical than ever, by supporting the candidature of Jules Grévy; by speaking eloquently at the celebrations for the Voltaire centenary; and by presiding at an international literary congress. It was too much, even for a Titan. During the night of 27/28 June 1878, in hot weather, after too copious a dinner and a violent argument (about a ceremony

Victor Hugo with
his grandchildren
Georges and Jeanne,
the heroes of *L'Art
d'être Grand-Père*

in honour of Rousseau and Voltaire) with little Louis Blanc, he had a very
slight stroke. Baucis – Juliette – begged him to leave for Guernsey as soon as
possible, and he finally agreed to do so, on 4 July.

Once there, he quickly recovered, but the hungry nymphs continued to
write to him. When the post arrived Juliette, who was staying at Hauteville
House itself this time, would see him hiding letters in his pockets.

He would sulk, snap at her, and call her a schoolmarm. In October she was
still undecided whether or not to follow Hugo to Paris, and proposed sharing
the solitude of Julie Chenay, the housekeeper at Hauteville House. Nevertheless
on 9 October the old lovers embarked together on the 'Diana'.

Meurice had rented for them a little town house, 130 avenue d'Eylau,
belonging to the Princesse de Lusignan. Lockroy's household, with Georges
and Jeanne, moved into No. 132, next door.

Victor Hugo in Guernsey during the summer of 1878

Due to the efforts of his disciples, fine collections of verse still appeared every year: in 1879 *La Pitié suprême*; in 1880 *Religions et Religion* and *L'Âne*; in 1881 *Les Quatre Vents de l'Esprit*; in 1882 *Torquemada*; in 1883 the last version of the *Légende des Siècles*. The world of letters, half rebellious and half admiring, was astonished by this fertile old age. In fact, all these poems were old ones.

In 1881 Victor Hugo's eightieth year was celebrated as a national holiday. A triumphal arch was built in the avenue d'Eylau, and on 26 February the people of Paris were invited to file past under the poet's windows. Many provincial towns sent delegations and flowers. The President of the Council, Jules Ferry, had come on the previous day to associate the government with this homage. All punishments were remitted in the lycées, the colleges and the primary schools. Standing at his open window, indifferent to the February cold, Victor Hugo, with Georges and Jeanne on each side of him, watched all day the passing of a procession of six hundred thousand admirers. A mountain of flowers sloped up from the roadway like an embankment. He expressed his gratitude with a priestly movement of the head.

In July the avenue d'Eylau was re-named avenue Victor-Hugo, and his friends were able to write to him: 'To Monsieur Victor Hugo, in his avenue.' On 14 July, there was another parade, of municipal bands, brass bands, and choirs, with *La Marseillaise*, which he liked, performed countless times. The celebration of 21 July, St Victor's Day, was a more intimate occasion. From 21 August to 15 September 1882, Juliette, his honorary, and now acknowledged mistress, stayed with Victor Hugo at Paul Meurice's house at Veules-les-Roses. On her return she had to go to bed. She was suffering from a malignant tumour of the digestive tract. In her old woman's face, hollowed by age, nothing remained of the dazzling beauty of 1830, unless it was the tender sweetness of her eyes and her finely shaped mouth.

It will be remembered that 22 November 1832 had been the first night of *Le Roi s'amuse*; and that it had not been possible to perform the play again because it had been banned. But to celebrate its fiftieth anniversary, Émile Perrin, manager of the Théâtre-Français, revived the play, and was particularly careful to make sure that the first night of the new production would fall on 22 November 1882. Juliette Drouet attended (the highest honour) with Victor

26 February 1881. Parisians filing past Victor Hugo's house in the avenue d'Eylau in honour of the poet's birthday

Juliette Drouet died
on 11 May 1883, aged
seventy-seven

Hugo, in the manager's box. The President of the Republic, Jules Grévy, occupied the stage box. After this ultimate tribute nothing was left for Juliette but to starve to death.

Of her approaching death she spoke as little as possible, although she knew her condition, because, according to Louis Guimbaud, Victor Hugo (like Goethe) insisted on people 'ridding themselves of their sorrows' and shaking off 'all traces of melancholy before they came to him'. At the dinners in the avenue d'Eylau, emaciated and almost unrecognizable, Juliette played sublimely the part that was demanded of her.

Death of Juliette　She died on 11 May 1883, aged seventy-seven. Victor Hugo had her interred at the Saint-Mandé cemetery, near the grave of Claire Pradier, under a tombstone that Juliette herself had chosen. Bowed down with sorrow, he was unable to leave the house where she had died to follow the funeral procession. Auguste Vacquerie, who took charge at all the Hugo funerals, spoke the oration: 'She, whom we mourn, was a valiant woman. . . .'

Hugo often intervened, no matter where it might be in the world, to save a condemned man, or to protect Jews from pogroms or rebels from repression. As an adolescent, Romain Rolland had kept an issue of *Don Quichotte* containing a coloured drawing of the aged Orpheus, with a halo of white hair, touching his lyre and raising his voice on behalf of the oppressed. He was a sort of French Tolstoy. 'He had appointed himself shepherd to the great flock of mankind.' He remained constant in his belief in immortality. On 31 August 1881 he wrote his will in a firm hand: 'God. The Soul. Responsibility. This threefold idea is

Victor Hugo as one of the 'Three Wise Men'. A painting by A. Gill ▶

sufficient for mankind. It has been sufficient for me. It is the true religion. I have lived in it. I die in it. Truth, light, justice, conscience: it is God. *Deus. Dies.*

'I leave forty thousand francs to the poor. And I wish to be taken to the cemetery in a pauper's hearse.

'My executors are MM. Jules Grévy, Léon Say, Léon Gambetta. They may co-opt whom they please. I leave all my manuscripts and everything which may be found written or drawn by myself to the Bibliothèque Nationale in Paris, which will one day become the Library of the United States of Europe.

'I leave behind me a sick daughter and two grandchildren. My blessing on them all.

'Apart from the eight thousand francs a year necessary for my daughter everything of mine belongs to my two grandchildren. I mention here, as sums which must be set aside, the annual income for life which I give to their mother Alice, and hereby increase to twelve thousand francs; and the annual income for life which I give to the courageous woman who at the time of the *coup d'état* saved my life at the risk of her own, and who subsequently saved the trunk containing my manuscripts.

'I shall close my earthly eyes, but my spiritual ones will remain open, wider than ever. I decline the prayers of all Churches. I ask for a prayer from every soul.

VICTOR HUGO.'

In a short codicil communicated to Auguste Vacquerie on 2 August 1883 he expressed the same ideas in a more abrupt and typical manner: 'I give fifty

Victor Hugo on his death-bed

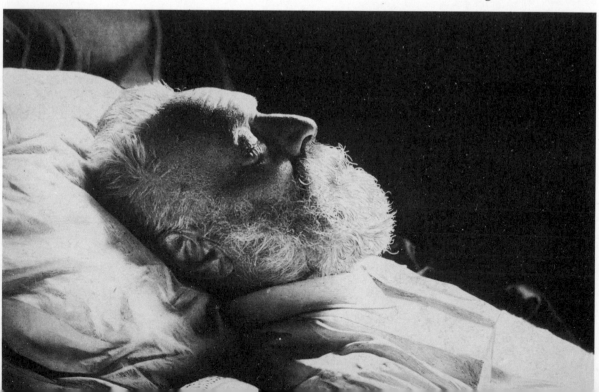

Victor Hugo

Victor Hugo's signature

thousand francs to the poor. I wish to be carried to the cemetery in their coffin. I refuse the prayers of all Churches; I ask for a prayer from every soul. I believe in God. – Victor Hugo.'

He used to say to his grandson: 'Love. . . . Try to find love . . . give happiness, and take it, in loving as much as you can.' But he knew that at his age neither pleasure nor fame provided a refuge from death. In his case the mortal accident was an attack of pneumonia, on 18 May 1885. He sensed that this was the end, and said to Paul Meurice, in Spanish: 'It will be very welcome.' It is wonderful that in this last delirium he should have composed one more perfect line: 'Here is the battleground of day and night.' It is a microcosm of his life, and of all lives.

He died on 22 May while bidding farewell to Georges and Jeanne. His last words, 'I see black light', are reminiscent of one of his best lines: 'That fearful black sun out of which spreads the darkness.' His death-rattle, said Georges Hugo, 'was like the sound of pebbles rolled by the waves of the sea'. A 'hurricane with thunder and hail, was unleashed on Paris as the old god suffered his final agony.'

On the news of his death, the Senate and Chamber of Deputies suspended their session as a sign of national mourning. It was decided that in this case the Panthéon would be put to the use for which the Constituent Assembly had intended it; that the inscription 'Aux grands hommes, la patrie reconnaissante' should be restored to the front of the building, and that the body of Victor Hugo should be buried there, after lying in state beneath the Arc de Triomphe.

'To know what this watch, kept by a whole city, was like,' says Barrès, 'one has to have seen it. One has to have seen the coffin towering in the dark of the night . . . while the greenish flames of the lamp-standards shone their sad light on the Imperial gateway, and were multiplied by their reflections in the breast-plates of the horsemen carrying torches, who were keeping the crowds in order. Huge waves of people, travelling from as far back as the place de la Concorde,

Death of
Victor Hugo

The Arc de Triomphe hung with crape on the evening of 31 May 1885. It was here that the poet lay in state

came to beat against the line of terrified horses, two hundred yards from the catafalque. The crowd was overcome with the knowledge that they had created a god. . . .'

A procession at once funereal and triumphant escorted Victor Hugo from the Étoile to the Panthéon. Two million Frenchmen followed the coffin. The avenues through which this human tide moved were flanked by masts bearing shields on which were displayed titles: *Les Misérables, Les Feuilles d'Automne, Les Contemplations, Quatrevingt-Treize.* In the street lamps, lit in broad daylight and draped with crape, pale flames flickered. For the first time in human history a nation was paying to a poet the tribute hitherto reserved by custom for sovereigns and military leaders.

The arrival of the funeral procession at the Panthéon ▶

1802 26 February: birth of Victor Hugo at Besançon.

1803 November: Mme Léopold Hugo moves to Paris with her three sons.

1807 October: Mme Hugo joins her husband, now Governor of the province of Avellino, in Italy. The Hugo children and their mother travel across France by stage-coach.

1809 February: Mme Hugo rents an apartment in Paris, at 12 impasse des Feuillantines, on the ground floor of the former convent founded by Anne of Austria.

1811 Spring: Mme Hugo and her sons join General Hugo at Bayonne and travel with him into Spain.

1814 September: General Hugo sends his sons Eugène and Victor to Cordier and Decotte's boarding-school in Paris.

1818 3 February: General Hugo and his wife legally separated. August: Eugène and Victor leave Cordier and Decotte's school and live with their mother at 18 rue des Petits-Augustins.

1819 26 April: Victor Hugo and Adèle Foucher declare their love for each other. December: the three Hugo brothers found a magazine, *Le Conservateur littéraire*.

1820 At the same time as writing 112 articles and 22 poems for his magazine in sixteen months, Hugo begins his first novel, *Han d'Islande*.

1821 January: Mme Hugo moves house to 10 rue de Mézières. March: *Le Conservateur littéraire* merges with *Les Annales de la Littérature et des Arts*. 27 June: death of Mme Hugo.

1822 June: publication of Hugo's first book, *Odes et Poésies diverses*. 12 October: Hugo marries Adèle Foucher at Saint-Sulpice.

1823 *Han d'Islande*. First edition in four volumes, without the author's name. 16 July: birth of Léopold Hugo II. 9 October: death of little Léopold.

1824 13 March: Victor Hugo publishes his *Nouvelles Odes*. The Hugos move to 90 rue de Vaugirard. 28 August: birth of Léopoldine Hugo.

1826 2 November: birth of Charles Hugo. April: the family moves to 11 rue Notre-Dame-des-Champs. *Odes et Ballades*.

1827 January: Hugo meets Sainte-Beuve. *Cromwell*. February: *Le Dernier Jour d'un Condamné*.

1828 21 October: birth of Victor Hugo, who in 1844 becomes François-Victor Hugo.

1829 January: *Les Orientales*. 14 July: the Théâtre-Français accepts *Marion Delorme*. 5 October: the Théâtre-Français accepts *Hernani* (completed on 25 September).

1830 25 February: first night of *Hernani*. May: the Hugos move to 9 rue Jean-Goujon.
28 July: birth of Adèle Hugo.

1831 January: Hugo finishes *Notre-Dame de Paris*.
November: *Les Feuilles d'Automne*.

1832 October: another move; this time to a large apartment at 6 place Royale, on the second floor of the Hôtel de Guéménée (now the Musée Victor Hugo).
22 November: first night of *Le Roi s'amuse*. It is banned the next day.

1833 16 February: beginning of liaison with Juliette Drouet.
Production of *Marie Tudor* at the Porte-Saint-Martin theatre.

1834 July: *Claude Gueux*.

1835 *Angelo, tyran de Padoue* performed at the Comédie-Française. Juliette leaves the Théâtre-Français without ever having played in it.
October: *Les Chants du Crépuscule*.

1836 February: Hugo an unsuccessful candidate for the Académie Française.

1837 *Les Voix intérieures*.
October: Victor Hugo writes *Tristesse d'Olympio* while on a solitary pilgrimage to the Bièvre valley.

1838 *Ruy Blas*, with Frédérick Lemaître in the title role, produced in a new theatre, the Renaissance (its director Anténor Joly was chosen by Hugo and Dumas).

1840 *Les Rayons et les Ombres*.

1841 7 January: Hugo elected to the Académie Française, at his fifth attempt.

1843 15 February: Léopoldine Hugo marries Charles Vacquerie.
7 March: *Les Burgraves* produced at the Comédie-Française. After its failure, Hugo ceases to write for the stage.
4 September: Léopoldine and her husband drowned at Villequier.

1844 Liaison with Léonie d'Aunet, wife of the painter Auguste Biard.

1845 13 April: Hugo raised to the peerage: Viscount Hugo.
5 July: at Auguste Biard's request, the Commissary of Police of the Vendôme district surprises Victor Hugo with Léonie d'Aunet.

1848 June: Hugo returned in the supplementary elections.
July: founds a newspaper, *L'Événement*.
13 October: The Hugo family moves into a magnificent house at 37 rue de la Tour d'Auvergne, Montmartre.

1849 Late October: *L'Événement* takes up a position against Louis-Napoleon.

1850 July: the editors of *L'Événement*, François-Victor and Charles Hugo, Paul Meurice, and Auguste Vacquerie, are imprisoned. *L'Événement* is banned but reappears under the title *L'Avènement du Peuple*.
11 December: Hugo leaves Paris under the name of Lanvin.
14 December: Juliette joins him in Brussels.

1852 1 August: Hugo, with Charles, leaves Belgium for St Helier.
Early August: *Napoléon le Petit*.
August: the family moves into Marine Terrace, St Helier.

1852–3 Winter: Hugo writes *Les Châtiments*.

1853–6 He writes *Les Contemplations, La Fin de Satan* and *Dieu*.

1855 31 October: Hugo leaves Jersey for Guernsey with François-Victor and Juliette Drouet.
2 November: Charles joins his father.

1856 April: *Les Contemplations* published. An extraordinary success; the first edition is sold out at once.
10 May: Hugo buys Hauteville House, Guernsey, with the proceeds of *Les Contemplations*.

1859 *La Légende des Siècles.*

1861 30 June: Hugo finishes *Les Misérables* (published in 1862).

1864 *William Shakespeare.*

1865 *Les Chansons des Rues et des Bois.*

1866 *Les Travailleurs de la Mer.*

1867 Revival of *Hernani.*

1868 27 August: death of Adèle Hugo. Hugo finishes *L'Homme qui rit.*

1869 May: first issue of *Le Rappel*, founded by the former editors of *L'Événement* and Henri Rochefort and Édouard Lockroy.
September: Victor Hugo goes to Lausanne to attend the Peace Conference.

1870 15 August: embarks for Belgium with Juliette, Charles and Alice Hugo, and their children.
5 September: Hugo returns to Paris.

1871 February: Hugo is elected to the National Assembly which is to sit at Bordeaux.
13 February: leaves for Bordeaux.
13 March: death of Charles at Bordeaux.

17 March: Hugo returns to Paris.
Late March: Victor Hugo leaves for Brussels to settle Charles' estate. He is soon expelled from Belgium and goes to Luxembourg.
Late September: returns to Paris.

1872 January: he is beaten in the elections.
20 February: revival of *Ruy Blas* at the Odéon, with Sarah Bernhardt in the role of the Queen.
7 August: departure for Guernsey.

1873 28 April: publication of *L'Année terrible. Quatrevingt-Treize* completed.
31 July: Hugo and Juliette return to France. The poet goes to live with his son in the avenue des Sycomores, Auteuil.
26 December: death of François-Victor Hugo.

1874 29 April: the family moves to 21 rue de Clichy.

1876 January: Victor Hugo is elected to the Senate.

1877 *L'Art d'être Grand-Père. La Légende des Siècles* (new version). *Histoire d'un Crime.*

1878 4 July: departure for Guernsey.
9 November: return to Paris. Hugo and Juliette move into 130 avenue d'Eylau.

1881 26 February: the beginning of Victor Hugo's eightieth year is celebrated as a national holiday.

1882 22 November: revival of *Le Roi s'amuse* at the Théâtre-Française.

1883 11 May: death of Juliette Drouet.

1885 22 May: death of Victor Hugo.
1 June: after lying in state beneath the Arc de Triomphe, the poet's body is interred in the Panthéon.

Frontispiece. This portrait of Victor Hugo is a lithograph after a drawing made by Maurin in 1829. *Photo Hachette*

Page

6 JOSEPH - LÉOPOLD - SIGISBERT HUGO, Victor Hugo's father, a general under the Empire, wrote madrigals, songs, and letters in the manner of Ronsard, also strange novels as black as night and thickly sown with catastrophes. This old warrior, though good-natured, gay, and an agreeable conversationalist, was subject to fits of depression

THE GENERAL'S WIFE (Sophie Françoise Trébuchet), the poet's mother, was born in 1772, the daughter of a ship's captain from Nantes. By 1793 she had become an ardent supporter of the Vendée revolt, which did not prevent her from marrying Major Léopold Hugo, of the 'Blue' (Republican) army. Nevertheless, she remained all her life a convinced Royalist.

7 MME TRÉBUCHET (born Lenormand du Buisson), Victor Hugo's maternal grandmother, was the daughter of a public prosecutor of the Presidial of Nantes who had consented to become a member of the Revolutionary Tribunal. *Photo Bulloz*

8 THE QUAI DE BATTANT must have looked in 1802, the year of Victor Hugo's birth, just as it does in this engraving, but the poet remembered nothing of his native town. Six weeks after he was born his father was ordered to leave Besançon for Marseilles. *Photo Hachette*

9 VICTOR HUGO'S BIRTHPLACE. Hugo was born in this seventeenth-century house on 26 February 1802. His father was at that time Battalion Commander of the 20th Half-Brigade at Besançon. *Photo Hurault-Viollet*

10 EUGÈNE HUGO, the poet's brother, born on 16 September 1800. He too was a writer, and he too later fell in love with Adèle Foucher. Subject to severe fits of depression, and shattered by his mother's death, he became insane after Victor's wedding. He died on 5 March 1837 at the Saint-Maurice asylum in Charenton.

ABEL, the eldest of the three Hugo brothers, born in 1798, took his role very seriously, and was of great help to the poet. He was extremely generous and concerned for his brother's success. *Photo Giraudon*

12 VICTOR HUGO, aged seventeen, from a miniature by Legénisel. It was at this time that Adèle Foucher and Victor declared their mutual love, and a correspondence began between them. In this period, too, thanks to Abel, Victor published an *Ode sur les Destins de la Vendée*, dedicated to Chateaubriand. *Photo Hachette*

13 THE HERMITAGE OF THE FEUILLANTINES, where in February 1809 Mme Hugo made her home in a huge ground-floor apartment. The drawing-room was of almost baronial proportions, the garden vast. Over the walls of this former convent founded by Anne of Austria, the dome of the Val-de-Grâce could be seen. It was here that Victor Hugo learnt to appreciate nature. *Photo Roger-Viollet*

14 IN A CARRIAGE LIKE THIS ONE in the

spring of 1811 Mme Hugo took her children to join their father in Spain. Little Victor was to retain a vivid memory of this journey, on which General Hugo's wife, now Countess of Siguenza, was treated with great respect. *Photo Hachette*

15 JOSEPH BONAPARTE, the man of letters transformed by an illustrious brother into a military figure, appreciated Mme Hugo's intelligence and was very ready to help the major. First he appointed him Governor of the province of Avellino. Later, when he himself was promoted from King of Naples to King of Spain and the Indies, he summoned Hugo to Madrid, and Léopold-Sigisbert became a general. *Photo Hachette*

17 THE COUR DU DRAGON. In September 1814 General Hugo placed his sons as boarders at Cordier and Decotte's school in Paris, in the rue Sainte-Marguerite, near the cour du Dragon. It was the end of their childhood. They were separated from their mother, whom they continued to idolize. They stayed here as boarders until August 1818. Already in 1817 Victor Hugo had received an honourable mention from the Académie Française for verses he had sent in for a poetry competition. *Photo Bulloz*

19 ADÈLE FOUCHER had been their playmate in the Feuillantines garden. Later Victor noticed her 'Infanta-like looks' and became very taken with her. Their love remained chaste until their marriage, which was solemnized at Saint-Sulpice on 12 October 1822, a year after Mme Hugo's death. *Photo Hachette*

PIERRE FOUCHER, the son of a shoemaker from Nantes, a friend of the Trébuchets, was a childhood friend of Sophie Hugo's. He became her family's best friend. Clerk to the Tribunal, he married Anne-Victoire Asseline, by whom he had four children. Adèle was his eldest daughter. *Photo Hachette*

21 'ODES ET POÉSIES DIVERSES' was the first book published by Hugo. In a grey-green cover, this volume, of which 1,500 copies were printed, first saw the light of day in June 1822, thanks once again to Abel's generosity. *Photo Hachette*

ETHEL AND ORDENER are the two main characters of *Han d'Islande*, Hugo's first novel, in which he expressed his love for Adèle. Begun several years before his marriage, *Han d'Islande* was published only in 1823, in four volumes, and without the author's name. *Photo Hachette*

22 VICTOR HUGO AGED TWENTY, from a pencil drawing attributed to Moitez. In the period between his mother's death and his own marriage the young Hugo lived in an attic in the rue du Dragon; but in the midst of his poverty he retained supreme dignity. *Photo Hachette*

23 THE HOUSE TAKEN BY THE FOUCHERS at Gentilly in the summer of 1822, to which Victor, henceforth accepted as Adèle's betrothed, was invited. To observe the proprieties, he slept in the pigeon-loft. He revelled in 'the happiness of Gentilly'. *Photo Giraudon*

24 MEDALLIONS BY DAVID D'ANGERS made after the marriage of Victor Hugo and Adèle Foucher. The Fouchers showed their understanding by offering to let the young couple stay with them in the Hôtel de Toulouse until Adèle and Victor could move into a flat of their own. *Photo Hachette*

25 THE TOWERS OF SAINT-SULPICE. At Cordier and Decotte's boarding-

school, where General Hugo's sons were sent after their parents' separation, Victor Hugo slept in a loft. From the end of 1816, even while preparing for his Polytechnique examinations, and following a course of study at the Lycée Louis-le-Grand, he was writing verse. From his window he could see the semaphore on the top of these towers. *Photo Hachette*

27 GENERAL HUGO'S HOUSE AT BLOIS, where Victor and Adèle's first son Léopold (born on 16 July 1823) and his nurse were sent. Léopold died on 9 October of the same year. In April 1825 Victor Hugo and Adèle stayed here. It was during this stay that he received news that he had been made a Chevalier of the Legion d'Honneur, and was invited to attend Charles X's coronation. *Photo Hachette*

29 MME VICTOR HUGO holding Léopoldine on her lap. A portrait by Devéria. The poet's eldest daughter, who was to become so dear to him, was born on 28 August 1824 in the flat at 90 rue de Vaugirard. *Photo Hachette*

30 'THE DREAM.' A pen-and-ink drawing by Hugo. It is one of a long series of drawings based on the writer's obsessions, anxieties and subconscious fantasies, as well as on particular subjects and impressions from his travels. *Photo Hachette*

FRONTISPIECE TO THE 1860 EDITION OF 'LES ORIENTALES'. 'Moonlight', an engraving by C. Cousin. Victor Hugo possessed a sense of the dramatic; and he tried to make each poem in this collection into a living scene. His inspiration, as far as the picturesque was concerned, came from the Bible, which he read and re-read at the Feuillantines, from advice given by an Orientalist, and,

above all, from his memories of Spain. *Photo Hachette*

31 MANUSCRIPT PAGE FROM 'ODES ET BALLADES'. On the publication of these poems in 1826 Victor Hugo was overjoyed to discover in *Le Globe*, a severe and important journal, a long and laudatory review of them by Sainte-Beuve. Goethe himself was not mistaken in his impression of this article, and Hugo's success with the younger generation was enormous. *Photo Hachette*

33 TALMA, the famous actor, never performed in any of Hugo's plays, but in the course of a dinner in 1826 the young writer explained his own ideas about the theatre to him, and told him how he wished to replace tragedy with drama. Talma was very interested in his *Cromwell*, but died shortly after this meeting. *Photo Hachette*

34 SAINTE-BEUVE quickly became a friend of the poet. Thanks to his intimacy with the Hugos, Sainte-Beuve felt for the first time in his life that he had been rescued from the solitary and sterile introspection which was characteristic of him. *Photo Hachette*

35 11 RUE NOTRE-DAME-DES-CHAMPS, the house into which the Hugo family moved in 1826. From its main entrance the poet could easily reach the city gates of Maine, Montparnasse, and Vaugirard, while an entrance at the bottom of the garden led to the Jardin du Luxembourg. Hugo was fond of both the house and the district. *Photo Giraudon*

36 PAUL FOUCHER, Victor Hugo's brother-in-law, was a member of the band of artists and poets which surrounded the young people in the Vaugirard quarter. It was under his name that Hugo's *Amy Robsart* – a

play based on Scott's *Kenilworth* – was performed at the Odéon in 1828. *Photo Hachette*

37 EUGÈNE DEVÉRIA. A portrait by his brother, Achille. Both were neighbours in the Vaugirard quarter; both were members of the Hugo's entourage; but they were always present at the evenings out and the dinners in the suburbs. *Photo Hachette*

DAVID D'ANGERS was a well-known sculptor when he became an intimate friend of the poet. At this period Hugo's discussions with his friends were as much to do with painting and sculpture as with poetry. *Photo Hachette*

38 ACHILLE DEVÉRIA was one of the greatest illustrators of the Romantic period. *Photo Hachette*

39 FRONTISPIECE TO 'BUG-JARGAL', designed by Devéria in 1826. *Bug-Jargal* is about the revolt in Santo Domingo. It was written in three weeks during the vacation of 1817, was reprinted by the publisher Gosselin. *Photo Roger-Viollet*

40 IN THE GREEN-ROOM OF THE COMÉDIE-FRANÇAISE, play-readings took place before the assembled associates. It was in such circumstances that on 14 July 1829, *Marion Delorme* was received with acclamation. Public taste had turned towards melodrama, and the Comédie-Française wished to present some. The censorship, however, banned *Marion*. *Photo Hachette*

41 ALFRED DE VIGNY and Victor Hugo had been friends since 1820. Alfred de Vigny was the poet's witness at his wedding. Three days after the reading of *Marion Delorme* at the Comédie-Française, de Vigny read his *More de Venise*, which was accepted by the company with equal enthusiasm. *Photo Hachette*

42 'THE IMMENSE CHURCH OF NOTRE-DAME squatting like a huge, two-headed Sphinx at the centre of the city' is the real hero of Hugo's novel. The poet knew the cathedral thoroughly. He was careful to make everything historically accurate: the scenery, the people and the language. *Photo Bulloz*

44 THÉOPHILE GAUTIER, in his pink doublet, was an ardent supporter at the first night of *Hernani*. From this moment 'good old Théo' became a faithful friend to whom Adèle, who was in charge of public relations, often had recourse. *Photo Hachette*

45 AT THE FIRST PERFORMANCE OF 'HERNANI', passionate supporters and hostile spectators came into vehement conflict. Before fighting each other on the barricades liberals and Royalists, Romantics and Classicists confronted each other in the theatre. *Photo Roger-Viollet*

46 CHARLES HUGO, born in November 1826, and two years younger than Léopoldine, was the elder of Victor Hugo's sons. While an adolescent he himself became a Hugoesque hero. He entered politics and spent some time in prison before joining his father in exile in Brussels. He married Alice Lehaene, later Mme Lockroy, and died suddenly at Bordeaux in March 1871. *Photo Hachette*

47 ADÈLE, born on 27 July 1830, took after her mother. She had a dreamy and melancholic temperament, and she suffered in exile because she was unable to find inner equilibrium in solitude. She died in 1915. These three drawings of Hugo's youngest children are the work of their mother. *Photo Hachette*

FRANÇOIS-VICTOR HUGO, born in October 1828, was, like his brother, a political journalist. He, too, was sent to prison, and released in January 1852 through the intervention of Louis-Napoleon. In exile he began the work of translating Shakespeare. He never married, and died in 1873. *Photo Hachette*

48 'NOTRE-DAME DE PARIS' was begun in 1829. The publisher Gosselin had a contract which promised him the novel that year, and he was inflexible. The July revolution obtained a respite for the author until February 1831, and Hugo finished this long novel in January 1831. It had taken him six months to write. *Photo Hachette*

49 THE CHARACTERS OF 'NOTRE-DAME DE PARIS' held a high place in Hugo's affections because of their bold personalities and their uncommon destinies. Although their 'Gothic' strangeness was very much in the Romantic taste, they are still popular today. Quasimodo, the deformed dwarf and victim of fate, and Esmeralda, a graceful vision rather than a woman, always accompanied by her familiar goat, are two of the principal characters of this great novel. *Photo Hachette*

50 'LES FEUILLES D'AUTOMNE' appeared in November 1831. Hugo wished to experience the same feelings as everyone else and to express himself better than anyone else. He succeeded: the resigned sadness which pervades this collection of poems was both surprising and touching. *Les Feuilles d'Automne* includes some of the finest poems ever written about children, about charity, and about the family.

51 IN 'LE ROI S'AMUSE' Victor Hugo dealt with one of the problems that was closest to his heart – injustice. The idea of this play came to him at Blois. Triboulet, Francis I's jester, had been born near General Hugo's house. The plot is a tissue of unlikely coincidences, relieved by a lively sense of dramatic effect and, here and there, by comic verve. *Photo Hachette*

52 6 PLACE ROYALE. The Hugos moved into the second floor of this noble house in October 1832. The rooms were vast and the walls covered in red damask. The flat was filled with Gothic and Renaissance furniture. At this time Hugo had nine dependants and he was also helping Eugène. His writing alone carried the weight of these outgoings. *Photo Hachette*

53 VICTOR HUGO. This drawing by Célestin Nanteuil shows Hugo in the year in which he moved to the place Royale. He was only thirty, but his face already bore the marks of his experience. Success had alienated his friends and increased the number of his enemies. Sainte-Beuve had betrayed his confidence and was writing a novel, *Volupté*, about his adventure with Adèle, colouring his adulterous love with vague mysticism. Victor Hugo's heart was empty and he was gloomy.

55 MLLE GEORGE, a deserter from the Comédie-Française, full of splendid memories of the Empire (she had been Napoleon's mistress), was still, at fifty, eager to play lovers' parts. She was appearing at this time at the Porte-Saint-Martin theatre, and was soon to play the title role in Victor Hugo's *Lucrèce Borgia*. *Archives Photographiques*

COSTUME DESIGNED FOR JULIETTE DROUET who played the part of the Princess Negroni in the first production of Hugo's *Lucrèce Borgia*. It was a small part, but the actress delighted the public. She was twenty-six and dazzlingly beautiful. *Photo Hachette*

57 'CONTEMPORARY ARTISTS.' This engraving of 1833 groups together Chateaubriand, Casimir Delavigne, Victor Hugo, Béranger, Alexandre Dumas, Lemercier, Lamartine, Étienne – an extraordinary mixture of generations and qualities. *Photo Bulloz*

58 LÉOPOLDINE. When Louis Boulanger made this pencil drawing of Léopoldine in 1837, the little girl was thirteen years old. She greatly admired her father, and was devoted to him. *Photo Giraudon*

59 JULIETTE DROUET, when she met the poet, was still seeking 'the passionate friendship of an upright man'. She understood Hugo's secret sufferings, lived only for him, and accepted for his sake an extremely difficult existence. *Photo Hachette*

60 THE DUC D'ORLÉANS, heir to the throne, and the hope of all who wanted a liberal policy on the part of the crown, married Princess Hélène of Mecklenburg in 1837. Victor Hugo, whose relations with the prince were better than with Louis-Philippe, was invited to their wedding banquet, an affair involving fifteen hundred guests. He was the young Duchesse d'Orléans' favourite poet; she had followed the literary life of France with passionate interest from the age of sixteen. *Photo Ellis*

61 FRÉDÉRICK LEMAÎTRE in the title role of *Ruy Blas* at its first production at the Renaissance. Maugin played Don Salluste, while the part of the Queen, which Victor Hugo had wanted to give to Juliette Drouet, was given to Mlle Baudoin, Frédérick Lemaître's mistress. A secret manœuvre on the part of Adèle Hugo, who was jealous, successfully influenced the theatre manager against complying with Hugo's wishes. Juliette took it very much to heart. *Photo Hachette*

62 'THE ACADÉMIE-FRANÇAISE STEEPLE-CHASE.' In this engraving by Granville, Victor Hugo, wearing Notre-Dame de Paris as a hat, and surrounded by his 'choirboys' (among whom are his brother-in-law Paul Foucher, Petrus Borel, and Arsène Houssaye), is shown with his rivals de Vigny, Alexandre Dumas, and Balzac. *Photo Giraudon*

63 VICTOR HUGO was elected to the Académie-Française on 7 January 1841, at his fifth attempt. His speech somewhat surprised his audience because he no longer disguised his political ambitions. *Photo Hachette*

64 VICTOR HUGO had his *Les Burgraves* produced in 1843. He hoped for another 'Battle of *Hernani*', but there was no second generation of Romantics and his grandiloquence bored Louis-Philippe's public. At the tenth performance the receipts fell to 1,666 francs, while Rachel, who was interpreting Racine, was making 5,500 francs for every performance. *Photo Giraudon*

65 'BURG À LA CROIX.' One of the free sketches which illustrate the Journal Hugo sent every evening to Adèle during his three journeys to the Rhine in 1838, 1839 and 1840. He felt a wish to understand and to write German poetry. He wrote that he had 'an almost filial feeling towards this noble country which is sacred to all thinkers'. *Photo Hachette*

66 LÉOPOLDINE HUGO MARRIED CHARLES VACQUERIE on 15 February 1843. He was the son of a Havre ship-fitter, who had built a large family house by the Seine at Villequier. The young people had intended to marry since 1839. In spite of his friendly feelings towards his future son-in-law, Hugo still had gloomy forebodings at the time of their marriage. *Photo Hachette*

68 CEMETERY AT VILLEQUIER where Charles and Léopoldine are buried in one coffin. The young couple were drowned at Villequier on 4 September 1843, in a boat in which Charles had won a first prize in the Honfleur regatta. *Photo Giraudon*

69 MANUSCRIPT OF 'À VILLEQUIER'. Léopoldine's death was a tremendous blow to Victor Hugo. He often went to Villequier, to the grave planted with roses. For years, on each 4 September, he wrote an anniversary poem, always beautiful in its tragic simplicity. *Photo Roger-Viollet*

70 LÉONIE D'AUNET had married a painter, Auguste Biard, in 1840. He ill-treated her. On Victor Hugo's side, compassion increased desire. In 1844, himself overwhelmed with grief, he became enamoured of Léonie. He sent her passionate letters, very similar to those he had recently written to Juliette. *Photo Hachette*

72 AFTER THE REVOLUTION OF FEBRUARY 1848, Victor Hugo was elected to the National Assembly. In July of the same year he founded a newspaper, *L'Événement*, to influence public opinion. Both in the Chamber and through his paper the poet was active, from the end of October 1848, in removing the obstacles in the way of Prince Louis-Napoleon's presidency. *Photo Hachette*

74 THIS POSTER FOR VICTOR HUGO was displayed on the walls of the capital during the supplementary elections of June 1848. The poet was elected. It was a sequel to his 'Letter to the Electors', posted during the April elections, in which Victor Hugo, without having officially offered himself as a candidate, nevertheless collected 60,000 votes. *Photo Hachette*

75 LOUIS-NAPOLEON achieved his *coup d'état* on 2 December 1851. Hugo had been a member of the opposition since October 1849. His integrity had caused him to break away from the policies of the Prince-President. At the time of the *coup d'état* he took an active part in the resistance, and Juliette courageously followed him in the midst of the disturbances. *Photo Bibliothèque Nationale*

77 LOUIS-NAPOLEON coldly and methodically pursued his plans from 1848 onwards. His objective was absolute power. His tactics were to gain control of the army and the police, and, during this operation, to keep the majority calm by pretending to be carrying out its policies. *Photo Hachette*

79 THE CONCIERGERIE. In July 1851 François-Victor Hugo, Paul Meurice and Auguste Vacquerie, editors of *L'Événement*, joined Charles Hugo who was imprisoned here. Victor Hugo himself was threatened, and on the day of the *coup d'état* the police came to his house to arrest him. Mme Hugo, although ill in bed, did not fail to keep in touch with the prisoners in the Conciergerie throughout the disturbances. *Photo Hachette*

81 16 GRANDE PLACE, BRUSSELS. After the *coup d'état* there was nothing to do but go into exile. On 11 December 1851 Victor Hugo left Paris. After several days in a Brussels hotel, he rented a sparsely furnished room at 16 Grande Place. He lived there for 100 francs a month and ate only one meal a day. *Photo Roger-Viollet*

82 1 AUGUST 1852. Having presided at an exiles' banquet, Victor Hugo, with Charles, left Belgium for Jersey. The island was like a bright green park scattered with neat little houses, with the sea at the base of tall cliffs like those at Lancon. *Photo Hachette*

83 MARINE TERRACE was the first house Victor Hugo lived in at the start of his exile in Jersey. This is where Mme Hugo joined him with their daughter Adèle and Auguste Vacquerie. Juliette had a small flat in a neighbouring cottage which bore the grandiose name of Nelson Hall. *Photo Hachette*

85 ILLUSTRATION FROM 'LES CHÂTIMENTS' (the Hetzel edition of 1872). After the success of *Napoléon le Petit* of which one million copies were circulated throughout the world, Victor Hugo, still inspired by indignation, wrote an admirable series of poems which he published in 1853 under the title of *Les Châtiments*. *Photo Hachette*

86 VICTOR HUGO, seated on the Exiles' Rock, seems himself to be illustrating the words of the cry which once burst from him: 'O send no one into exile! O exile is impious!' In a hundred forms the idea of proscription, now melancholy, now triumphant, had dominated his thought. *Photo Hachette*

87 A VIEW OF GUERNSEY sketched by Georges-Victor Hugo. At the end of October 1855, after Queen Victoria's alliance with Napoleon III against Russia, Hugo was forced to leave Jersey for Guernsey. The family lived at the island's capital, St Peter's Port, and rented a house at the end of a rocky promontory.

88 AUGUSTE VACQUERIE, Léopoldine's brother-in-law and the faithful companion of Mme Hugo, who had looked after him in 1836 when he was alone and ill as a student in Paris, went with the family into exile. This photograph shows him with Victor Hugo in Guernsey. *Photo Hachette*

89 HAUTEVILLE HOUSE, which Victor Hugo bought with the 20,000 francs he received for *Les Contemplations*, a collection of poems published in 1856. There was little hope of any rapid change in the situation in France, and the writer had no wish to leave Guernsey, where his work was going well and his health was excellent. *Photo Levy*

90 AT HAUTEVILLE HOUSE the Hugos regularly organized meals for the poor children of the island. Mme Hugo is shown on the left in the photograph. On the right are Paul Chenay, the engraver who married Julie Foucher, Mme Hugo's younger sister; Hennet de Kesler, a proscript; and Victor Hugo. *Photo Hachette*

91 VICTOR HUGO'S TWO SONS, Charles and François-Victor, shared their father's exile. In 1859 they went with their mother and their sister Adèle to England. Then, in 1862, Charles went back to Paris without giving his father any warning. François-Victor, who was working hard at his Shakespeare translation, was less troubled by exile than were the others. He became engaged to an island girl, Emily de Putron, who was consumptive. She died in January 1865. After this loss, he left the island. *Photo Hachette*

THE OAK GALLERY of Hauteville House. Hugo arranged the house and its furniture to reflect his own personality. A whole house full of panelling, chests, pillars, and heavy furniture with Gothic carving gave visitors the impression of stepping into a Rembrandt engraving. These trappings were as grandiose and Romantic as the master of the house himself. *Photo Lévy*

92 IN 'LA LÉGENDE DES SIÈCLES' Victor Hugo sought 'to express humanity in a kind of cyclic work'. On its publication in Paris the collection won

admiration from even the most un-willing quarters. *Photo Hachette*

93 GENERAL HUGO, the hero of *Après la Bataille*, from *La Légende des Siècles*. A painting by Melingue. *Photo Encyclopedie par l'Image*

DEDICATION PAGE of Paul Meurice's copy of *La Légende des Siècles*. This drawing was made on 1 January 1860 by Victor Hugo, at Hauteville House. *Photo Hachette*

94 VICTOR HUGO, at fifty-nine, already had the bushy, patriarchal look which was to be the aspect of him remembered by history. Ever since he began to suffer from a stubborn malady of the throat, which he took to be tuberculosis of the larynx, Hugo had allowed his beard to grow. *Photo Hachette*

MME VICTOR HUGO stayed away from Jersey as long as she could. In 1861 she was away from March to December. In 1862 and 1863 there were similar absences. After her son Charles's wedding she stayed in Brussels for two years, from 1865 to 1867. *Photo Pierre Petit*

96 'LES MISÉRABLES' appeared in July 1862. The manuscript had been completed a year earlier. Victor Hugo had a taste for the extreme, the theatrical and the exaggerated. In this work these excesses are justified by the true and noble feelings it contains. His respect for and horror of Javert were authentic, and so was his love for Jean Valjean. As human beings his characters are quite extraordinary, but from the point of view of art, though monsters, they have lasting validity because they are beautiful.

97 GAVROCHE AGED ELEVEN. A pen-and-ink drawing by Victor Hugo. Sainte-Beuve, who was not always interested in masterpieces, did not write an article about *Les Misérables*, but set down in the secrecy of his *Notebooks* that while everyone else of his own generation had become old, Victor Hugo had just given dazzling proof of his youth. *Photo Hachette*

98 IN 'LES TRAVAILLEURS DE LA MER', published in 1866, rocks and monsters were painted realistically. As for the heroes, Gilliatt and Deruchette, they belonged to the author's own private mythology. There were also comic-opera smugglers and traitors belonging to the world of melodrama. This novel brought the octopus into fashion. *Photo Roger-Viollet*

99 END OF THE BREAKWATER, Guernsey. During his whole stay in the Channel Islands, Hugo kept an account of disasters caused by the sea. He used the knowledge he acquired while living in the islands in his novel *Les Travailleurs de la Mer*.

101 FOR THE 1867 EXPOSITION UNIVER-SELLE, it was decided to stage a revival of *Hernani* in Paris. It was a tremendous triumph, both in literary terms and as a political demonstration. The receipts from it could not have been higher (seven thousand gold francs). Mme Hugo, in spite of a severe illness, insisted on attending the dress rehearsal. *Photo Hachette*

103 POSTER ISSUED BY THE COMMUNE. Victor Hugo was in Brussels settling the estate of his son Charles, who had just died, when the Commune was set up. He did not approve of its excesses, but he begged the Versailles government not to respond to violence with cruelty. The Versailles government entered Paris on 21 May 1871; on the 23rd, this notice was posted on the walls. The repression was severe in the extreme. *Photo Hachette*

104 GUNS IN MONTMARTRE. Victor Hugo returned from exile on 5 September 1870. The Emperor had just capitulated. From the train which was bringing him back from Brussels he saw the first harassed and discouraged soldiers of the retreating French army. The old man wept. As soon as he arrived in Paris he wrote an 'Appeal to the Germans', on which he placed high hopes; but the fighting drew nearer; soon Paris was being besieged, and there were guns in Montmartre itself. *Photo Bulloz*

105 DURING THE SIEGE there was a great famine. The Parisians ate dogs, cats and rats, bought from butchers and poulterers who had nothing else to offer. *Photo Hachette*

107 29 JANUARY 1871. The armistice was signed and a National Assembly was elected to negotiate peace. It was to sit at Bordeaux. Victor Hugo stood as a candidate for the Seine district and left for Bordeaux on 13 February. The Assembly which was elected did not reflect his Republican and patriotic sympathies. *Photo Hachette*

108 CHARLES HUGO and his family accompanied the poet to Bordeaux, and on 13 March Hugo's elder son died of an attack of apoplexy. His body was brought back to Paris. Along the whole route of the funeral procession battalions of the National Guard presented arms. Barricades necessitated long detours. Paris was in open revolt; the Commune was taking power.

109 THE HÔTEL DE VILLE WAS BURNT on 24 May, after the Versailles government had entered Paris. In Brussels every day Victor Hugo heard news of a death or an arrest. The journalists Rochefort and Henry Bauer were in prison; Louise Michel, 'the Red Virgin' whose 'formidable compassion' aroused Hugo's admiration, was in danger of her life. *Photo Hachette*

110 HUGO IN 1872. After all his experiences since first going into exile, Victor Hugo felt worn out. In the Paris of 1872 influential people hated him for his political views. In January he was defeated in the elections; in February his unfortunate daughter Adèle, who had become insane, came back to Paris to be confined there. *Photo Hachette*

111 HUGO'S HOUSE IN VIANDEN. A drawing by Victor Hugo. After the Commune Hugo decided to go and live in Luxembourg for the time being. He knew the little town of Vianden, having stopped there on one of his journeys with Juliette. *Photo Paul Géniaux*

112 SARAH BERNHARDT as the Queen in the Odéon production of *Ruy Blas*. Standoffish at first, she treated the poet as a mere 'amnestied Communard', but the young actress was soon conquered and could refuse the 'dear monster' nothing. *Photo Carjat*

113 JUDITH GAUTIER, Théophile Gautier's daughter, who had married the poet Catulle Mendès, was another young beauty who fell victim to the attractions of the seventy-year-old 'maître'. *Photo Chéri Rousseau*

115 TO WRITE 'QUATREVINGT-TREIZE' Victor Hugo retired to Hauteville House. He left for Guernsey in August 1872, and started the novel in November. When he returned to Paris on 31 July of the following year *Quatrevingt-Treize* was completed. It was published in 1874. In describing the supermen who were the heroes of his book, even his

faults as a writer came in useful. *Photo Roger-Viollet*

116 'LES PLACARDS POPULAIRES', a publication intended to introduce to the public at large 'the most interesting and well-loved men' of the age, began its series with biographical studies of Victor Hugo and his two sons, Charles-Victor and François-Victor. *Photo Hachette*

119 HUGO WITH JEANNE AND GEORGES, the heroes of *L'Art d'être Grand-Père* (published in 1877). He was extremely fond of his son Charles' children and he spoiled them. He had rather unusual ideas about education; he insisted that his daughter-in-law allow these children, young as they were, to stay up for all the dinner-parties. *Photo Bulloz*

120 HUGO IN 1878. During his stay at Hauteville House from 1872 to 1873 Victor Hugo had an affair with a twenty-two-year-old sewing-maid, Blanche, whom Mme Drouet had unwisely engaged. The affair continued in Paris, to the scandal of Juliette and the rest of Hugo's intimates. This liaison was still alive when, after a slight stroke, the poet returned for the last time to Hauteville House in the summer of 1878.

121 26 FEBRUARY 1881. The beginning of Victor Hugo's eightieth year was celebrated as a national occasion. Standing between his two grandchildren, at a first-floor window, Victor Hugo watched the procession of his admirers, who had come from all over the country to lay flowers in front of his house in the avenue d'Eylau, which in July 1881 became the avenue Victor-Hugo.

122 JULIETTE DROUET died of a malignant tumour of the digestive tract on 11 May 1883. On the fiftieth anniversary of their meeting, in February 1883, Victor Hugo gave her a photograph of himself with the inscription: 'Fifty years of love is the best marriage of all.' She had been an example of complete sacrifice to a redeeming love. *Photo Hachette*

123 VICTOR HUGO AS ONE OF THE 'THREE WISE MEN'. A painting by A. Gill. This was how a large part of the public saw him. The poet had defended justice and liberty all his life. He was the glory of French literature, a kind of national hero. *Photo Giraudon*

124 VICTOR HUGO DIED ON 22 MAY 1885. It is said that a hurricane, with thunder and hail, was unleashed on Paris at the moment of his final agony. *Photo Nadar*

125 VICTOR HUGO'S SIGNATURE. *Photo Hachette*

126 THE ARC DE TRIOMPHE DRAPED IN BLACK. Here the poet lay in state on 31 May 1885, the eve of his funeral. Twelve young French poets formed a guard of honour, and there was an enormous crowd. *Photo Hachette*

127 HUGO'S FUNERAL PROCESSION. It was decided that, in Hugo's honour, the Panthéon would be used for the purpose prescribed for it by the Constituent Assembly. The inscription 'Aux grands hommes, la patrie reconnaissante' was restored to the front of the building. The body of the poet was interred there on 1 June 1885. Two million Frenchmen followed the funeral.

INDEX

Numbers in italics refer to the illustrations